STEAKS, CHOPS, ROASTS & RIBS

STEAKS, CHOPS, ROASTS & RIBS

Packed with delicious recipes for the oven and barbecue

p

This is a Parragon Book
First published in 2006

Parragon
Queen Street House
4 Queen Street
Bath BA1 1HE
United Kingdom

This edition designed by Talking Design Ltd, Worthing, West Sussex

Photography and text by The Bridgewater Book Company Ltd

ISBN: 1-40544-889-X

Printed in China

NOTE
This book uses metric and imperial measurements. Follow the same units of measurement throughout; do not mix metric and imperial. All spoon measurements are level: teaspoons are assumed to be 5 ml and tablespoons are assumed to be 15 ml. Unless otherwise stated, milk is assumed to be full fat, eggs and individual vegetables such as potatoes are medium, and pepper is freshly ground black pepper.

The times given for each recipe are an approximate guide only because the preparation times may differ accordingly to the techniques used by different people and the cooking times may vary as a result of the type of oven and other equipment used.

Recipes using raw or very lightly cooked eggs should be avoided by infants, the elderly, pregnant women, convalescents and anyone suffering from an illness. Pregnant and breast-feeding women are advised to avoid eating peanuts and peanut products.

CONTENTS

INTRODUCTION

Even in prehistoric times, meat formed part of the human diet, especially once people had mastered the art of making fire and could therefore cook it to make it more tender and palatable. Almost every cuisine across the globe includes some meat dishes, although some have cultural or religious constraints about eating particular animals. In the West, meat constitutes a major part of the diet and tender, distinctive cuts, such as steaks and chops, are generally more highly prized than the cheaper cuts that require long, slow cooking to render them edible.

For many people, a meal that doesn't include such recognizable cuts of meat simply isn't a proper meal. Others, who eat meat occasionally rather than every day, like their carnivorous option to be a bit of a treat, something that

they can "get their teeth into"– roast lamb or sirloin steak, for example. It's human nature to push the boat out when entertaining guests or cooking for special occasions and celebrations, so we tend to buy more luxurious ingredients and that includes the best cuts of meat, such as fillet of beef. After all, why miss the opportunity to indulge in Festive Beef Wellington (see page 160) even if you have to live on sausages and pasta for the rest of the month?

Of course, not all these cuts will break the family budget. Pork, for example, is usually quite an economical buy, whether chops for grilling, a leg or a piece of gammon for roasting or ham steaks for griddling. Although it may be more difficult to carve, many people consider shoulder of lamb to have the sweetest and most tender meat yet it is a much less expensive cut than leg. No barbecue will ever be complete without a rack of ribs, a wonderfully inexpensive and messy delight.

This book is packed with recipes for cooking steaks, chops, roasts and ribs of all kinds – from veal to venison – and offers useful advice and guidance on buying, storing and handling meat. And, to make the meal complete, the final chapter provides some great ideas for side dishes to serve as accompaniments.

NUTRITION

In recent years, red meat has had a bad press and its consumption has been blamed for a wide variety of medical conditions, some of them life-threatening. This is simplistic and not really justified, as these problems are generally caused by over-indulgence – eating any food to excess, even carrots, can cause health problems. Cooking techniques also have a role to play in the healthy diet. Griddled or grilled chops are certainly healthier options than pan-fried and it is also sensible to give some thought to accompaniments. Steak and chips may be a classic combination, but it's the latter that really increases the unhealthy fat content of the meal. Once in a while is fine, but there are lots of other tasty possibilities.

Meat is a valuable source of protein and what's more it's high quality protein that contains the essential eight amino acids, which the human body cannot synthesize itself. Protein is vital for good health and plays an important role in the growth, maintenance and repair of the body's cells. As an approximate guide, the protein content of grilled, griddled or roasted lean cuts is as follows:

100 g/3^1/$_2$ oz beef	27–29 g/1–1^1/$_8$ oz protein
100 g/3^1/$_2$ oz lamb	23–29 g/^{3}/$_4$–1^1/$_8$ oz protein
100 g/3^1/$_2$ oz pork	26–30 g/1–1^1/$_4$ oz protein
100 g/3^1/$_2$ oz veal	31 g/1^1/$_4$ oz protein
100 g/3^1/$_2$ oz venison	35 g/1^3/$_8$ oz protein

The body requires relatively small amounts of protein and nutritionists recommend that protein-rich foods should constitute only 12 per cent of the daily diet. In effect, this means 55 g/2 oz for adult men, 40 g/1½ oz for adult women and 28 g/1^1/$_8$ oz for children aged between seven and ten.

Most people are now aware that a diet high in fats, especially saturated fat, is the cause of many health problems, from obesity to heart disease. In the last fifty years, meat producers have bred animals that have become progressively leaner. Some meats now contain less than half the fat that was typical in the 1950s and even pork, which was once considered excessively fatty, now sometimes needs basting during cooking to prevent it from drying out. As an approximate guide, the fat content of grilled, griddled or roasted lean cuts is as follows:

100 g/3^1/$_2$ oz beef	4–12 g/^{1}/$_8$–^{1}/$_2$ oz fat
100 g/3^1/$_2$ oz lamb	8–12 g/^{3}/$_{10}$–^{1}/$_2$ oz fat
100 g/3^1/$_2$ oz pork	6–10 g/^{1}/$_5$–^{1}/$_2$ oz fat
100 g/3^1/$_2$ oz veal	12 g/^{1}/$_2$ oz fat
100 g/3^1/$_2$ oz venison	6 g/^{1}/$_5$ oz fat

Some fat – about 25 g/1 oz – is necessary in the diet. Most of the fat in meat is saturated and nutritionists recommend that this should make up no more than 10 per cent of an adult's daily intake of calories. This is because these fats increase the level of blood cholesterol which can lead to medical conditions such as heart disease. Cholesterol present in food is not thought to have any effect on blood cholesterol levels.

Meat does not contain dietary fibre or carbohydrates. However, it is a source of some important minerals and vitamins – iron, zinc, magnesium, niacin, riboflavin (vitamin B2), thiamine (vitamin B1) and vitamin B12.

Buying meat

Whatever type of meat you are buying, it is important to select the right cut for the cooking method and recipe you have chosen. Suitable cuts for roasting, grilling, griddling and frying are the ones that come from the back of the animal where the muscles have had to do the least amount of work – the saddle, loin and fillet, for example. Legs and shoulders may also be roasted.

Meat should always smell pleasant and look attractive. The surface should be slightly moist, but not damp or slimy. So-called white meat should be pinkish in colour, while red meat, particularly beef, should be dark red rather than crimson. Very young veal is pinkish-grey in colour. Any fat should be fairly soft in texture and white or creamy coloured, not yellow.

Beef: Although it is tempting to buy small, neat, boneless cuts, such as topside for roasting because they look attractive and are easy to carve, these are best kept for pot-roasting. The best roasting cuts are from the ribs, fillet, back and sirloin. Both fore rib and middle rib are available boned and rolled, but prime rib is usually sold on the bone and is regarded as one of the best roasting cuts. Rolled ribs are easier to carve, but standing ribs look more impressive.

For frying, griddling and grilling, buy tender steaks such as fillet, sirloin, porterhouse, T-bone, rib eye, entrecôte and rump. Flank steak, sometimes known as London broil, varies in tenderness but can be an economical choice.

Lamb: Unlike beef, which is taken from a mature animal, lamb comes from animals of less than a year old, usually about six to seven months. This results in tender meat and smaller cuts. Interestingly, there is currently a movement towards reinstating that nineteenth-century favourite, mutton, which comes from the mature sheep. Older lamb, known as hogget, is popular in some parts of the world, particularly Australia and New Zealand.

Several cuts are suitable for roasting. The leg, weighing 1.8–2.7 kg/4–6 lb, is a popular choice. It is also commonly sold divided into two pieces – the knuckle or shank and the leg fillet. Rack of lamb, also known as best end of neck, is an economical cut for roasting, ideal for serving two or three people. It is also used to make a guard of honour – two racks placed, fat side out, facing each other with the ribs interlocked – and crown roast – two racks formed into a round, fat side facing in, with the central cavity filled with stuffing. Both of these look very appetizing and are a good choice for entertaining. The saddle or loin is extremely tender and is the most expensive cut. Weighing up to 3.6 kg/8 lb, it is a magnificent and impressive cut for entertaining. Smaller cuts from the loin are also suitable for roasting and these may be boned and rolled. Shoulder and half shoulder are quite fatty cuts but the meat is very sweet.

There are several kinds of chops, including loin, chump and best end of neck cutlets. Lamb steaks are usually taken from the leg fillet.

Pork: Like lamb, pork comes from the young animal, so the meat is tender and there is a wide choice of quality cuts. As the leg (ham) is so big, it is usually cut into two pieces, both of which may be roasted. Similarly, the loin is usually divided into the hind or rear and fore or front loin, but the whole loin, weighing up to 5.5 kg/12 lb may be roasted if you are entertaining a large number of guests. The tenderloin, also known as pork fillet, may be roasted or pan-fried.

Chops are cut from the loin and may include loin, fore loin and chump chops. Sparerib chops, taken from the shoulder, are not so tender as those from the loin, but are succulent and less expensive. Ribs or spare ribs are taken from the belly and are usually sold in sheets for cooking on the barbecue or in Chinese sauces.

Veal: Veal is very tender, offering a wide choice of cuts. The leg, loin and rib may all be roasted and the shoulder is often boned and rolled for roasting. Chops, fillets and escalopes from the leg are usually pan-fried, but Florentine chops, the equivalent of the beef T-bone steak, can be grilled.

STORING AND HANDLING MEAT

Always store meat in the refrigerator – it is best placed on the bottom shelf to prevent any juices from dripping onto other foods and contaminating them. Keep raw meat completely separate from cooked foods. If it's pre-packed, as it is in many supermarkets, simply place the pack on a plate before putting in the refrigerator. Otherwise, wrap it in foil and place on a plate first. Beef, lamb and mutton will keep for 3–5 days and pork and veal will keep for 2–4 days. Chops and steaks will go off more rapidly than roasts. Always observe the use-by date on the packaging.

To avoid cross-contamination, it is sensible to keep a chopping board specifically for meat and never use it for vegetables or other ingredients. Polythene is better than wood as it can be sterilized and is dishwasher safe. Wash your hands and any kitchen tools, such as knives, after handling raw meat before touching other raw or cooked ingredients.

MARINADES

Red Wine Marinade

Makes about 175 ml/6 fl oz

Preparation time: 5 minutes

150 ml/5 fl oz cup full-bodied red wine

1 tbsp red wine vinegar

1 tbsp olive oil

2 garlic cloves, finely chopped

2 bay leaves, torn

pepper

Whisk together all the ingredients in a jug and season with pepper. Pour over red meat or venison, cover and leave to marinate for up to 12 hours.

White Wine Marinade

Makes about 300 ml/10 fl oz

Preparation time: 5 minutes

225 ml/8 fl oz dry white wine

6 tbsp olive oil

2 tbsp freshly squeezed lemon juice

3 tbsp finely chopped fresh flat-leaf parsley

1 tbsp snipped fresh chives

pepper

Whisk together all the ingredients in a jug and season with pepper. Pour over chops, cover and leave to marinate for up to 12 hours.

Madeira Marinade

Makes about 250 ml/9 fl oz

Preparation time: 5 minutes, plus 30 minutes standing

6 tbsp freshly squeezed orange juice

175 ml/6 fl oz Madeira

4 shallots, finely chopped

grated rind of ½ orange

salt and pepper

Whisk together all the ingredients in a jug and season with salt and pepper. Leave to stand for 30 minutes to allow the flavours to mingle. Pour over any meat, cover and leave to marinate for up to 12 hours.

Marinade with Juniper Berries

Makes about 500 ml/18 fl oz

Preparation time: 5 minutes

500 ml/18 fl oz red wine

1 shallot, sliced

5 juniper berries, crushed

salt and pepper

Pour the wine into a shallow dish and add the onion and juniper berries. Season with salt and pepper and add pork or veal, turning to coat. Cover and leave to marinate for 5–12 hours, stirring occasionally.

1

STEAKS

Grilled , griddled, pan-fried or cooked on a barbecue, steaks of all sorts are always popular but if served completely plain, they can be rather dull and unexciting. This chapter is packed with recipes for making the most of these tender cuts with marinades, salsas, relishes and sauces to enhance their texture and flavour. Naturally, beef steaks take pride of place with a surprising variety of fabulous ways to cook them from Sozzled Sirloin (see page 38) to Ginger Beef with Chilli (see page 62). But there are lots of other choices too, including lamb, ham, pork and even venison.

TABASCO STEAKS WITH WATERCRESS BUTTER

1 BUNCH OF WATERCRESS

85 G/3 OZ UNSALTED BUTTER, SOFTENED

4 SIRLOIN STEAKS, ABOUT 225 G/8 OZ EACH

4 TSP TABASCO SAUCE

SALT AND PEPPER

SERVES 4

Preheat the barbecue. Using a sharp knife, finely chop enough watercress to fill 4 tablespoons. Reserve a few watercress leaves for the garnish. Place the butter in a small bowl and beat in the chopped watercress with a fork until fully incorporated. Cover with clingfilm and leave to chill in the refrigerator until required.

Sprinkle each steak with 1 teaspoon of the Tabasco sauce, rubbing it in well. Season to taste with salt and pepper.

Cook the steaks over hot coals for 2½ minutes each side for rare, 4 minutes each side for medium and 6 minutes each side for well done. Transfer to serving plates, garnish with the reserved watercress leaves and serve immediately, topped with the watercress butter.

Alternative Cooking Method
A griddle pan or frying pan can also be used to cook this steak. Ensure that you brush the pan with a little oil first and then pre-heat before adding the meat. Cooking times may be increased slightly as this method of cooking does not generate the high heat of a barbecue. You therefore will need to look for visual signs that the food is cooked to your liking.

SPICY LAMB STEAKS

4 LAMB STEAKS,
ABOUT 175 G/6 OZ EACH
8 FRESH ROSEMARY SPRIGS
8 FRESH BAY LEAVES
2 TBSP OLIVE OIL

SPICY MARINADE

2 TBSP SUNFLOWER OIL
1 LARGE ONION, FINELY CHOPPED
2 GARLIC CLOVES, FINELY
CHOPPED
2 TBSP JERK SEASONING
1 TBSP CURRY PASTE
1 TSP GRATED FRESH
ROOT GINGER
400 G/14 OZ CANNED CHOPPED
TOMATOES
4 TBSP WORCESTERSHIRE SAUCE
3 TBSP LIGHT MUSCOVADO SUGAR
SALT AND PEPPER

SERVES 4

To make the marinade, heat the oil in a heavy-based saucepan. Add the onion and garlic and cook, stirring occasionally, for 5 minutes, or until softened. Stir in the jerk seasoning, curry paste and grated ginger and cook, stirring constantly, for 2 minutes. Add the tomatoes, Worcestershire sauce and sugar, then season to taste with salt and pepper. Bring to the boil, stirring constantly, then reduce the heat and simmer for 15 minutes, or until thickened. Remove from the heat and leave to cool.

Place the lamb steaks between 2 sheets of clingfilm and beat with the side of a rolling pin to flatten. Transfer the steaks to a large, shallow, non-metallic dish. Pour the marinade over them, turning to coat. Cover with clingfilm and leave to marinate in the refrigerator for 3 hours.

Preheat the barbecue. Drain the lamb, reserving the marinade. Cook the lamb over medium hot coals, brushing frequently with the marinade, for 5–7 minutes on each side. Meanwhile, dip the rosemary and bay leaves in the olive oil and cook on the barbecue for 3–5 minutes. Serve the lamb immediately with the herbs.

Alternative Cooking Method
A griddle pan or frying pan can also be used to cook this steak. Ensure that you brush the pan with a little oil first and then pre-heat before adding the meat. Cooking times may be increased slightly as this method of cooking does not generate the high heat of a barbecue. You therefore will need to look for visual signs that the food is cooked to your liking.

GRIDDLED STEAK WITH
HOT CHILLI SALSA

4 SIRLOIN STEAKS,
ABOUT 225 G/8 OZ EACH
SUNFLOWER OIL, FOR BRUSHING
SALT AND PEPPER

FOR THE SALSA
4 FRESH RED HABANERO OR
SCOTCH BONNET CHILLIES
4 FRESH GREEN POBLANO CHILLIES
3 TOMATOES, PEELED,
DESEEDED AND DICED
2 TBSP CHOPPED FRESH CORIANDER
1 TBSP RED WINE VINEGAR
2 TBSP OLIVE OIL

SERVES 4

First make the salsa. Preheat the grill. Arrange the chillies on a baking sheet and cook, turning frequently, until blackened and charred. Leave to cool, then rub off the skins with kitchen paper. Halve and deseed the chillies, then chop finely.

Mix the red and green chillies, tomatoes and coriander together in a bowl. Blend the vinegar and oil together in a jug, season with salt and pour over the salsa. Toss well, cover and chill in the refrigerator until required.

Season the steaks with salt and pepper. Brush a griddle pan lightly with oil and heat over a medium heat until hot. Cook the steaks for 2–4 minutes on each side, or until cooked to your liking. Serve immediately with the salsa.

GLAZED GAMMON STEAKS

4 GAMMON STEAKS

4 TBSP DARK BROWN SUGAR

2 TSP MUSTARD POWDER

4 TBSP BUTTER

8 SLICES PINEAPPLE

TO SERVE

BAKED POTATO AND GREEN BEANS

SERVES 4

Preheat the griddle over a medium heat, place the gammon steaks on it and cook for 5 minutes, turning once. If you have room for only two steaks at a time, cook them completely and keep warm while cooking the second pair.

Combine the brown sugar and mustard in a small bowl.

Melt the butter in a large frying pan, add the pineapple and cook for 2 minutes to heat through, turning once. Sprinkle with the sugar and mustard and continue cooking over a low heat until the sugar has melted and the pineapple is well glazed. Turn the pineapple once more so that both sides are coated with sauce.

Place the gammon steaks on individual plates and arrange 2 pineapple slices either next to them or overlapping on top. Spoon over some of the sweet pan juices.

Serve with a baked potato and green beans.

MEXICAN STEAK WITH
AVOCADO SALSA

4 BEEF STEAKS

3 TBSP SUNFLOWER OIL,
PLUS EXTRA FOR OILING

½ RED ONION, GRATED

1 FRESH RED CHILLI,
DESEEDED AND FINELY CHOPPED

1 GARLIC CLOVE, CRUSHED

1 TBSP CHOPPED FRESH CORIANDER

½ TSP DRIED OREGANO

1 TSP GROUND CUMIN

AVOCADO SALSA

1 RIPE AVOCADO

GRATED RIND AND JUICE OF 1 LIME

1 TBSP SUNFLOWER OIL

½ RED ONION, CHOPPED FINELY

1 FRESH RED CHILLI,
DESEEDED AND FINELY CHOPPED

1 TBSP CHOPPED FRESH CORIANDER

SALT AND PEPPER

SERVES 4

Using a sharp knife, make a few cuts in the edge of fat around each steak. Place the meat in a shallow, non-metallic dish.

Mix the sunflower oil, onion, chilli, garlic, coriander, oregano and cumin together in a small bowl. Pour the marinade over the steaks, turning the meat so that it is well coated. Cover and leave to marinate in the refrigerator for 1–2 hours.

Preheat the barbecue. To make the salsa, halve the avocado and remove the stone. Peel and cut the flesh into small dice. Place the avocado, lime rind and juice, sunflower oil, onion, chilli, coriander and salt and pepper to taste in a bowl and mix well. Cover and leave to chill in the refrigerator until required.

Cook the steaks on an oiled rack over hot coals for 6–12 minutes on each side. Serve the steaks accompanied with the avocado salsa.

Alternative Cooking Method

A griddle pan or frying pan can also be used to cook this steak. Ensure that you brush the pan with a little oil first and then pre-heat before adding the meat. Cooking times may be increased slightly as this method of cooking does not generate the high heat of a barbecue. You therefore will need to look for visual signs that the food is cooked to your liking.

PORK STEAKS WITH LEMON-GRASS

MARINADE

2 GARLIC CLOVES, CRUSHED

½ TSP FRESHLY GROUND BLACK PEPPER

1 TBSP SUGAR

2 TBSP FISH SAUCE

2 TBSP SOY SAUCE

1 TBSP SESAME OIL

1 TBSP LIME JUICE

2 LEMON-GRASS STALKS, OUTER LEAVES REMOVED, CHOPPED FINELY

4 SPRING ONIONS, CHOPPED FINELY

2 TBSP COCONUT MILK

4 PORK STEAKS

TO GARNISH

LIME WEDGES

TO SERVE

SALAD OR STIR-FRIED VEGETABLES

SERVES 4

To make the marinade, place the garlic, pepper, sugar, fish sauce, soy sauce, sesame oil, lime juice, lemon-grass, spring onions and coconut milk in a large shallow dish and mix well to combine.

Turn the pork steaks in the marinade, cover the dish with clingfilm and place in the refrigerator for 1 hour.

Grill the pork steaks under a preheated grill or over charcoal, for 5 minutes on each side, or until cooked through. Garnish with lime wedges and serve with salad or stir-fried vegetables.

STEAKS IN ORANGE SAUCE

2 LARGE ORANGES

25 G/1 OZ BUTTER

4 FILLET STEAKS,
ABOUT 175 G/6 OZ EACH

6 TBSP BEEF STOCK

1 TBSP BALSAMIC VINEGAR

SALT AND FRESHLY GROUND
BLACK PEPPER

TO GARNISH

FRESH PARSLEY LEAVES

SERVES 4

Cut the oranges in half, then cut off 4 thin slices and reserve for the garnish. Squeeze the juice from the remaining orange halves.

Melt the butter in a heavy-based frying pan. Add the steaks and cook for 1–2 minutes on each side or until browned and sealed. Remove from the pan, season to taste with salt and pepper, set aside and keep warm.

Pour the orange juice into the pan and add the beef stock and vinegar. Simmer over a low heat for 2 minutes. Season the orange mixture to taste with salt and pepper and return the steaks to the pan. Heat through gently for about 2 minutes or according to taste. Serve immediately, garnished with the reserved orange slices and the parsley.

BEEF WITH WILD
MUSHROOM

4 BEEF STEAKS

50 G/1¾ OZ BUTTER

1–2 GARLIC CLOVES, CRUSHED

150 G/5½ OZ MIXED
WILD MUSHROOMS

2 TBSP CHOPPED FRESH PARSLEY

TO SERVE

SALAD LEAVES AND
CHERRY TOMATOES, HALVED

SERVES 4

Preheat the barbecue. Place the steaks on to a chopping board and using a sharp knife, cut a pocket into the side of each steak.

To make the stuffing, heat the butter in a large frying pan. Add the garlic and fry gently for 1 minute. Add the mushrooms to the frying pan and sauté gently for 4–6 minutes, or until tender. Remove the frying pan from the heat and stir in the parsley.

Divide the mushroom mixture into 4 and insert a portion into the pocket of each steak. Seal the pocket with a cocktail stick. If preparing ahead, allow the mixture to cool before stuffing the steaks.

Cook the steaks over hot coals, searing the meat over the hottest part of the barbecue for 2 minutes on each side. Move the steaks to an area with slightly less intense heat and barbecue for a further 4–10 minutes on each side, depending on how well done you like your steaks.

Transfer the steaks to serving plates and remove the cocktail sticks. Serve with salad leaves and cherry tomatoes.

Alternative Cooking Method

A griddle pan or frying pan can also be used to cook this steak. Ensure that you brush the pan with a little oil first and then pre-heat before adding the meat. Cooking times may be increased slightly as this method of cooking does not generate the high heat of a barbecue. You therefore will need to look for visual signs that the food is cooked to your liking.

PEPPER STEAK

2 TBSP BLACK OR
MIXED DRIED PEPPERCORNS,
COARSELY CRUSHED

4 FILLETS STEAKS,
ABOUT 2.5 CM/1 INCH THICK,
AT ROOM TEMPERATURE

15 G/½ OZ BUTTER

1 TSP SUNFLOWER OIL

4 TBSP BRANDY

4 TBSP CRÈME FRAÎCHE OR
DOUBLE CREAM (OPTIONAL)

SALT AND PEPPER

TO GARNISH

WATERCRESS LEAVES

SERVES 4

Spread out the crushed peppercorns on a plate and press the steaks into them to coat on both sides.

Melt the butter with the oil in a large sauté or frying pan over a medium-high heat. Add the steaks in a single layer and cook for 3 minutes on each side for rare; 3½ minutes on each side for medium-rare; 4 minutes on each side for medium; and 4½–5 minutes on each side for well done.

Transfer the steaks to a warmed plate and set aside, covering with foil to keep warm. Pour the brandy into the pan to deglaze, increase the heat and use a wooden spoon to scrape any sediment from the base of the pan. Continue boiling until reduced to around 2 tablespoons.

Stir in any accumulated juices from the steaks. Spoon in the crème fraîche, if using, and continue boiling until the sauce is reduced by half again. Taste, and adjust the seasoning if necessary. Spoon the pan sauce over the steaks, garnish with the watercress and serve at once.

NEAPOLITAN PORK STEAKS

4 PORK LOIN STEAKS,
EACH ABOUT 125 G/4½ OZ

SERVES 4

SAUCE

2 TBSP OLIVE OIL

1 GARLIC CLOVE, CHOPPED

1 LARGE ONION, SLICED

400 G/14 OZ CANNED TOMATOES

2 TSP YEAST EXTRACT

75 G/2¾ OZ BLACK OLIVES, STONED

2 TBSP SHREDDED FRESH BASIL

TO GARNISH

FRESH BASIL LEAVES, FRESHLY
GRATED PARMESAN CHEESE

TO SERVE

FRESHLY COOKED VEGETABLES
AND FRESH ITALIAN BREAD

To make the sauce, heat the oil in a large frying pan. Add the garlic and onion and cook, stirring, for 3–4 minutes or until they just begin to soften.

Add the canned tomatoes and yeast extract to the frying pan and simmer for about 5 minutes or until the sauce starts to thicken.

Cook the pork steaks under a preheated grill for 5 minutes on both sides until the meat is cooked through. Set the pork aside and keep warm.

Going back to the sauce, add the olives and fresh shredded basil and stir quickly to combine.

Transfer the steaks to warm serving plates. Top with the sauce, sprinkle with basil and Parmesan and serve with cooked vegetables and fresh Italian bread.

NEW ORLEANS STEAK
SANDWICH

4 TBSP OLIVE OIL

2 LARGE ONIONS,
SLICED THINLY INTO RINGS

2 GARLIC CLOVES, CHOPPED

1 TBSP RED WINE VINEGAR

1 TBSP CHOPPED FRESH THYME

3 TBSP CHOPPED FRESH PARSLEY

2 TSP PREPARED MILD MUSTARD

SALT AND PEPPER

4 RUMP STEAKS,
ABOUT 175 G/6 OZ EACH

8 SLICES SOURDOUGH OR
CRUSTY BREAD

115 G/4 OZ ROQUEFORT CHEESE,
CRUMBLED

4 TOMATOES, SLICED

1 LITTLE GEM LETTUCE,
SHREDDED

SERVES 4

Heat half the oil in a heavy-based frying pan. Add the onions and garlic, sprinkle with a pinch of salt, then cover and cook over a very low heat for 25–30 minutes, or until very soft and caramelized.

Process the onion mixture in a food processor until smooth. Scrape into a bowl, stir in the vinegar, thyme, parsley and mustard and season with salt and pepper. Cover and place at the side of the barbecue.

Brush the steaks with the remaining oil and season with salt and pepper. Grill on a hot barbecue for 2 minutes on each side for rare, 4 minutes on each side for medium or 6 minutes on each side for well done.

Meanwhile, toast the bread on both sides. Spread the onion mixture on the toast. Slice the steaks and top 4 toast slices with the meat. Sprinkle with the crumbled Roquefort, then add the tomatoes and lettuce leaves. Top with the remaining toast and serve.

Alternative Cooking Method

A griddle pan or frying pan can also be used to cook this steak. Ensure that you brush the pan with a little oil first and then pre-heat before adding the meat. Cooking times may be increased slightly as this method of cooking does not generate the high heat of a barbecue. You therefore will need to look for visual signs that the food is cooked to your liking.

PORK STEAKS WITH MUSTARD AND APPLE

2 EATING APPLES, PEELED,
CORED AND GRATED
55 G/2 OZ FRESH WHOLEMEAL
BREADCRUMBS
1 TBSP CHOPPED FRESH SAGE
2 TSP WHOLEGRAIN MUSTARD
4 PORK STEAKS
OLIVE OIL, FOR BRUSHING

TO GARNISH

WEDGES OF LEMON AND
A SMALL SALAD

SERVES 4

Mix together the grated apples, breadcrumbs, sage and mustard in a bowl. Trim any visible fat from the pork steaks and brush with oil.

Grill the pork steaks over a medium barbecue for 6–7 minutes. Remove the steaks from the barbecue, transfer to a board and turn them over. Press the topping firmly over them, then grill for a further 10–15 minutes.

Carefully transfer the steaks to serving plates, topping-side up, garnish with lemon wedges and a small salad and serve immediately.

Alternative Cooking Method

A griddle pan or frying pan can also be used to cook this steak. Ensure that you brush the pan with a little oil first and then pre-heat before adding the meat. Cooking times may be increased slightly as this method of cooking does not generate the high heat of a barbecue. You therefore will need to look for visual signs that the food is cooked to your liking.

SOZZLED SIRLOIN

6 SIRLOIN STEAKS,
ABOUT 175 G/6 OZ EACH

SERVES 6

MARINADE

175 ML/6 FL OZ GUINNESS

2 TBSP SUNFLOWER OIL

3 TBSP DARK BROWN SUGAR

2 TBSP WORCESTERSHIRE SAUCE

1 TBSP WHOLEGRAIN MUSTARD

2 GARLIC CLOVES,
FINELY CHOPPED

MUSTARD BUTTER

225 G/8 OZ BUTTER, SOFTENED

2 TBSP TARRAGON MUSTARD

1 TBSP CHOPPED FRESH PARSLEY

Place the steaks in a large, shallow dish. Mix together the Guinness, sunflower oil, sugar, Worcestershire sauce, wholegrain mustard and garlic in a jug. Pour the mixture over the steaks, turning to coat. Cover with clingfilm and marinate in the refrigerator for 4 hours.

Meanwhile, beat together the butter, mustard and parsley in a bowl until combined. Cover and chill until required.

Drain the steaks, reserving the marinade. Grill on a hot barbecue, brushing frequently with the marinade, for 2 minutes on each side for rare, 4 minutes on each side for medium or 6 minutes on each side for well done. Serve immediately, topped with the mustard butter.

Alternative Cooking Method

A griddle pan or frying pan can also be used to cook this steak. Ensure that you brush the pan with a little oil first and then pre-heat before adding the meat. Cooking times may be increased slightly as this method of cooking does not generate the high heat of a barbecue. You therefore will need to look for visual signs that the food is cooked to your liking.

CHARGRILLED VENISON STEAKS

4 VENISON STEAKS

SERVES 4

MARINADE

150 ML/5 FL OZ RED WINE

2 TBSP SUNFLOWER OIL

1 TBSP RED WINE VINEGAR

1 ONION, CHOPPED

FEW SPRIGS OF FRESH PARSLEY

2 SPRIGS OF FRESH THYME

1 BAY LEAF

1 TSP CASTER SUGAR

½ TSP MILD MUSTARD

SALT AND PEPPER

TO SERVE

JACKET POTATOES, SALAD LEAVES
AND CHERRY TOMATOES

VARIATION

FOR A VARIATION ON THIS
RED WINE MARINADE,
SEE PAGE 10

Place the venison steaks in a shallow, non-metallic dish.

To make the marinade, combine the wine, oil, wine vinegar, onion, fresh parsley, thyme, bay leaf, sugar and mustard, and salt and pepper to taste in a bowl or screw-top jar. Stir or shake vigorously until well combined. Alternatively, using a fork, whisk the ingredients together in a bowl.

Pour the marinade mixture over the venison, cover, and leave to marinate in the refrigerator overnight. Turn the steaks over in the mixture occasionally so that the meat is well coated.

Cook the venison over hot coals, sealing the meat over the hottest part of the barbecue for about 2 minutes on each side.

Move the meat to an area with slightly less intense heat and cook for another 4–10 minutes on each side, depending on how well done you like your steaks.

Serve with jacket potatoes, salad leaves and cherry tomatoes.

Alternative Cooking Method
A griddle pan or frying pan can also be used to cook this steak. Ensure that you brush the pan with a little oil first and then pre-heat before adding the meat. Cooking times may be increased slightly as this method of cooking does not generate the high heat of a barbecue. You therefore will need to look for visual signs that the food is cooked to your liking.

MUSTARD STEAKS WITH
TOMATO RELISH

4 SIRLOIN OR RUMP STEAKS

1 TBSP TARRAGON MUSTARD

2 GARLIC CLOVES, CRUSHED

TOMATO RELISH

225 G/8 OZ CHERRY TOMATOES

55 G/2 OZ MUSCOVADO SUGAR

50 ML/2 FL OZ WHITE WINE
VINEGAR

1 PIECE OF STEM GINGER,
CHOPPED

½ LIME, THINLY SLICED

SALT

TO GARNISH

FRESH TARRAGON SPRIGS

SERVES 4

To make the tomato relish, place all the ingredients in a heavy based saucepan, seasoning to taste with salt. Bring to the boil, stirring until the sugar has completely dissolved. Reduce the heat and simmer, stirring occasionally, for 40 minutes, or until thickened. Transfer to a bowl, cover with clingfilm and leave to cool.

Preheat the barbecue. Using a sharp knife, cut almost completely through each steak horizontally to make a pocket. Spread the mustard inside the pockets and rub the steaks all over with the garlic. Place them on a plate, cover with clingfilm and leave to stand for 30 minutes.

Cook the steaks over hot coals for 2½ minutes each side for rare, 4 minutes each side for medium or 6 minutes each side for well done. Transfer to serving plates, garnish with fresh tarragon sprigs and serve immediately with the tomato relish.

Alternative Cooking Method
A griddle pan or frying pan can also be used to cook this steak. Ensure that you brush the pan with a little oil first and then pre-heat before adding the meat. Cooking times may be increased slightly as this method of cooking does not generate the high heat of a barbecue. You therefore will need to look for visual signs that the food is cooked to your liking.

GAMMON IN MADEIRA
SAUCE

4 GAMMON STEAKS,
ABOUT 225 G/8 OZ EACH

25 G/1 OZ BUTTER

2 CLOVES

1 MACE BLADE

225 ML/8 FL OZ MADEIRA

2 TSP MEAUX MUSTARD

TO GARNISH

FRESH FLAT-LEAF
PARSLEY SPRIGS

VARIATION

FOR A VARIATION ON THIS
MADEIRA SAUCE,
SEE PAGE 10

SERVES 4

Snip the edges of the gammon steaks with kitchen scissors to prevent them from curling up as they cook.

Melt the butter in a large, heavy-based frying pan, then add the cloves and mace blade. Add the gammon, in batches if necessary, and cook for 3 minutes on each side. Transfer to a warmed dish, cover and keep warm.

Add the Madeira to the frying pan and bring to the boil, stirring and scraping up any sediment from the base of the frying pan. Stir in the mustard and cook for 2 minutes, or until the sauce is thickened and glossy. Pour the sauce over the gammon, garnish with parsley sprigs and serve immediately.

TEQUILA-MARINATED
BEEF STEAKS

2 TBSP OLIVE OIL

3 TBSP TEQUILA

3 TBSP FRESHLY SQUEEZED
ORANGE JUICE

1 TBSP FRESHLY SQUEEZED LIME
JUICE

3 GARLIC CLOVES, CRUSHED

2 TSP CHILLI POWDER

2 TSP GROUND CUMIN

1 TSP DRIED OREGANO

SALT AND PEPPER

4 SIRLOIN STEAKS

SERVES 4

Place the oil, tequila, orange and lime juices, garlic, chilli powder, cumin, oregano and salt and pepper to taste in a large, shallow, non-metallic dish and mix together. Add the steaks and turn to coat in the marinade. Cover and leave to chill in the refrigerator for at least 2 hours or overnight, turning occasionally.

Preheat the barbecue and oil the grill rack. Let the steaks return to room temperature, then remove from the marinade. Cook over hot coals for 3–4 minutes on each side for medium, or longer according to taste, basting frequently with the marinade. Serve immediately.

Alternative Cooking Method

A griddle pan or frying pan can also be used to cook this steak. Ensure that you brush the pan with a little oil first and then pre-heat before adding the meat. Cooking times may be increased slightly as this method of cooking does not generate the high heat of a barbecue. You therefore will need to look for visual signs that the food is cooked to your liking.

RUMP STEAK WITH DARK
BARBECUE SAUCE

2 TBSP SUNFLOWER OIL

MARINADE

1 ONION, FINELY CHOPPED

450 G/1 LB TOMATOES, PEELED,

DESEEDED AND CHOPPED

2 TBSP LEMON JUICE

1 TBSP TABASCO SAUCE

2 TBSP WORCESTERSHIRE SAUCE

2 TBSP MUSCOVADO SUGAR

1 TSP MUSTARD POWDER

140 G/5 OZ SHALLOTS,

FINELY CHOPPED

140 G/5 OZ BUTTER, SOFTENED

6 RUMP STEAKS,

ABOUT 175 G/6 OZ EACH

SALT AND PEPPER

TO GARNISH

A FEW SPRIGS OF WATERCRESS

SERVES 6

Heat the oil in a large frying pan. Cook the onion over a low heat, stirring occasionally, for 5 minutes, or until softened. Stir in the tomatoes, lemon juice, Tabasco and Worcestershire sauces, sugar and mustard powder. Cover and simmer, stirring occasionally, for 15–20 minutes, or until thickened. Pour into a large dish and leave to cool.

Meanwhile, blanch the shallots in boiling water for 2–3 minutes. Drain well and pat dry with kitchen paper. Place in a food processor and process to a purée. Gradually work in the butter and season with salt and pepper. Scrape the shallot butter into a bowl, cover and chill until required.

Add the steaks to the cooled marinade, turning to coat. Cover and marinate in a cool place for 4 hours.

Drain the steaks, reserving the marinade. Grill on a hot barbecue, brushing frequently with the marinade, for 2 minutes on each side for rare, 4 minutes on each side for medium or 6 minutes on each side for well done. Serve each steak topped with a spoonful of shallot butter and garnish with watercress sprigs.

Alternative Cooking Method

A griddle pan or frying pan can also be used to cook this steak. Ensure that you brush the pan with a little oil first and then pre-heat before adding the meat. Cooking times may be increased slightly as this method of cooking does not generate the high heat of a barbecue. You therefore will need to look for visual signs that the food is cooked to your liking.

STEAK WITH COUNTRY GRAVY

4 RUMP STEAKS,
ABOUT 140 G/5 OZ EACH
125 G/4½ OZ PLAIN FLOUR
PINCH OF CAYENNE PEPPER,
OR TO TASTE
3–4 TBSP RENDERED BACON FAT
OR SUNFLOWER OR GROUNDNUT OIL
300 ML/10 FL OZ FULL-FAT MILK
OR SINGLE CREAM
SALT AND PEPPER

SERVES 4

Put the steaks between pieces of greaseproof paper and use a rolling pin to beat them until they are about 5 mm/¼ inch thick. Set aside.

Put the flour onto a large plate and season with cayenne pepper and salt and pepper to taste. Dust the steaks with the seasoned flour on both sides, shaking off any excess, and reserve the leftover flour.

Heat 3 tablespoons of the bacon fat in a large frying pan over a medium-high heat. Add as many steaks as will fit without overcrowding the pan and cook for 5–6 minutes, turning once, until they are cooked through as desired and are crisp and brown on the outside. Transfer the steaks to a plate and keep warm in a low oven while cooking the remaining steaks, if necessary. Add more fat to the pan as needed.

To make the country gravy, put 5 tablespoons of the reserved seasoned flour into a small bowl, slowly stir in half the milk and continue stirring until no lumps remain.

Pour off all but about 1 tablespoon of the fat in the frying pan. Pour the milk mixture into the pan, stirring to scrape up the sediment. Pour in the remaining milk and bring to the boil. Reduce the heat and simmer for 2 minutes, stirring constantly, to remove the raw flour taste. Taste and adjust the seasoning, if necessary. Serve the steaks with the gravy poured over.

BOOZY BEEF STEAKS

4 BEEF STEAKS

4 TBSP WHISKY OR BRANDY

2 TBSP SOY SAUCE

1 TBSP DARK MUSCOVADO SUGAR

PEPPER

TOMATO SLICES

TO GARNISH

FRESH PARSLEY SPRIGS

TO SERVE

GARLIC BREAD

SERVES 4

Make a few cuts in the edge of fat on each steak. This will stop the meat curling as it cooks. Place the meat in a shallow, non-metallic dish.

Mix the whisky, soy sauce, sugar and pepper to taste together in a small bowl, stirring until the sugar dissolves. Pour the mixture over the steak. Cover with clingfilm and leave to marinate in the refrigerator for at least 2 hours. Preheat the barbecue. Cook the meat over hot coals, searing the meat over the hottest part of the barbecue for 2 minutes on each side.

Move the meat to an area with slightly less intense heat and cook for a further 4–10 minutes on each side, depending on how well done you like your steaks. To test if the meat is cooked, insert the point of a sharp knife into the meat – the juices will run from red when the meat is still rare, to clear as it becomes well cooked.

Lightly barbecue the tomato slices for 1–2 minutes. Transfer the meat and the tomatoes to warmed serving plates. Garnish with fresh parsley sprigs and serve with garlic bread.

Alternative Cooking Method

A griddle pan or frying pan can also be used to cook this steak and tomato dish. Ensure that you brush the pan with a little oil first and then pre-heat before adding the meat. Cooking times may be increased slightly as this method of cooking does not generate the high heat of a barbecue. You therefore will need to look for visual signs that the food is cooked to your liking.

STEAK WITH BLUE CHEESE TOPPING

MARINADE

150 ML/5 FL OZ RED WINE

1 TBSP RED WINE VINEGAR

1 TBSP OLIVE OIL

1 GARLIC CLOVE, FINELY CHOPPED

1 BAY LEAF, CRUMBLED

1 TBSP WHOLEGRAIN MUSTARD

4 RUMP OR SIRLOIN STEAKS,
ABOUT 175 G/6 OZ EACH

55 G/2 OZ BLUE CHEESE,
SUCH AS GORGONZOLA

55 G/2 OZ FRESH WHITE
BREADCRUMBS

2 TBSP CHOPPED FRESH PARSLEY

TO GARNISH

A SMALL SALAD

SERVES 4

Mix together the red wine, vinegar, olive oil, garlic, bay leaf and mustard in a shallow dish. Add the steaks, turning to coat, then cover and leave in a cool place to marinate for 4 hours.

Meanwhile, mix together the blue cheese, breadcrumbs and parsley in a small bowl. Cover and store in the refrigerator until required.

Drain the steaks. Grill for 2 minutes on each side for rare, 4 minutes on each side for medium or 6 minutes on each side for well done. Spoon the cheese topping onto the steaks, pressing it down with the back of the spoon, when you turn the steaks. Serve immediately, garnished with a small salad.

STEAK PARCELS

4 SIRLOIN OR RUMP STEAKS

300 ML/10 FL OZ DRY RED WINE

2 TBSP OLIVE OIL

SALT AND PEPPER

25 G/1 OZ BUTTER

2 TSP DIJON MUSTARD

4 SHALLOTS, FINELY CHOPPED

4 FRESH THYME SPRIGS

4 BAY LEAVES

VARIATION

FOR A VARIATION ON THIS
RED WINE MARINADE,
SEE PAGE 10

SERVES 4

Place the steaks in a large, shallow, non-metallic dish. Mix the wine and oil together in a jug and season to taste with salt and pepper. Pour the marinade over the steaks, cover with clingfilm and leave to marinate in the refrigerator for up to 8 hours.

Preheat the barbecue. Cut out 4 squares of foil large enough to enclose the steaks and coat the centres with the butter and mustard. Drain the steaks and place them on the foil squares. Top with the shallots, thyme and bay leaves and fold over the foil to make neat parcels.

Cook the parcels over hot coals for 10 minutes, turning once. Serve the steaks immediately in the parcels.

Alternative Cooking Method

Preheat the oven to 180°C / 350°F. Cook the steaks in their parcels for 15-20 mins, checking after 10 mins to see if the steak is cooked to your liking.

PORK IN WHITE WINE AND OLIVE SAUCE

1 TSP OLIVE OIL

1 BONELESS PORK STEAK

¼ TSP DRIED OREGANO

¼ TSP DRIED THYME

SALT AND PEPPER

2 TSP LEMON JUICE

4 TBSP DRY WHITE WINE

4 TBSP WATER

6 BLACK OLIVES

TO SERVE

RICE OR FRESH PASTA

VARIATION

FOR A VARIATION ON THIS WHITE WINE SAUCE, SEE PAGE 10

SERVES 1

Sprinkle oil over the pork steak. Rub in the herbs and salt and pepper to season.

Heat a non-stick frying pan and brown the pork quickly over a high heat, turning once.

Pour over the lemon juice, wine and water. Bring to the boil, then reduce the heat, cover and simmer gently for 15 minutes.

Add the olives to the pan and continue cooking for a further 5 minutes to heat through.

Serve with rice or fresh pasta.

BEEF WITH PEPPER AND TOMATOES

2 TBSP PLAIN FLOUR

SALT AND PEPPER

1 VERY THIN ENTRECÔTE OR
SIRLOIN STEAK

1 TBSP OLIVE OIL

1 TBSP UNSALTED BUTTER

SAUCE

½ SMALL RED PEPPER, DICED

2 TOMATOES, SKINNED AND DICED

50 ML/2 FL OZ DRY WHITE WINE

2 TBSP LEMON JUICE

SERVES 1

Season the flour with salt and pepper. Dredge the steak in the flour, shaking off any excess.

Heat the oil over a high heat in a large frying pan. When it is sizzling, add the butter and cook until melted. Swirl the pan around to combine the oil and butter.

Cook the steak in the pan over a high heat for 1–2 minutes depending on the thickness, then turn and cook the other side for 1–2 minutes. The meat should not be too rare for this dish.

Transfer the cooked steak to a warm serving dish. Scrape the bottom of the frying pan with a wooden spoon to incorporate any bits that have stuck to the bottom.

Add the diced pepper and tomatoes to the pan and mix well. Stir in the wine and lemon juice. Bring to the boil, reduce the heat and simmer gently for 2 minutes. Pour over the steak and serve.

GINGER BEEF WITH CHILLI

4 LEAN BEEF STEAKS,
SUCH AS RUMP, SIRLOIN OR
FILLET, 100 G/3½ OZ EACH
2 TBSP GINGER WINE
2.5 CM/1 INCH PIECE OF FRESH
ROOT GINGER, FINELY CHOPPED
1 GARLIC CLOVE, CRUSHED
1 TSP GROUND CHILLI
1 TSP VEGETABLE OIL
SALT AND PEPPER

RELISH

225 G/8 OZ FRESH PINEAPPLE
1 SMALL RED PEPPER
1 FRESH RED CHILLI
2 TBSP LIGHT SOY SAUCE
1 PIECE OF STEM GINGER IN
SYRUP, DRAINED AND CHOPPED

TO GARNISH

FRESH RED CHILLI STRIPS

TO SERVE

FRESHLY COOKED NOODLES AND
2 SPRING ONIONS, SHREDDED

SERVES 4

Trim any excess fat from the steaks if necessary. Using a meat mallet or covered rolling pin, pound the steaks until they are 1 cm/½ inch thick. Season on both sides with salt and pepper to taste and place in a shallow dish.

Combine the ginger wine, fresh root ginger, garlic and chilli and pour over the meat. Cover with clingfilm and chill for 30 minutes.

Meanwhile, make the relish. Peel and finely chop the pineapple and place it in a bowl. Halve, deseed and finely chop the pepper and chilli. Stir into the pineapple with the soy sauce and stem ginger. Cover with clingfilm and chill until required.

Brush a ridged grill pan with the oil and heat until very hot. Drain the beef and add to the pan, pressing down to seal. Lower the heat and cook for 5 minutes. Turn the steaks over and cook for a further 5 minutes.

Drain the steaks on kitchen paper and transfer to warmed serving plates. Garnish with chilli strips and serve with noodles, spring onions and the relish.

STEAKS WITH RED ONION

4 RUMP STEAKS

2 TSP WHOLEGRAIN MUSTARD

SALT AND PEPPER

2 TBSP SUNFLOWER OIL

GRATED RIND AND

JUICE OF ½ ORANGE

RED ONION MARMALADE

2 TBSP OLIVE OIL

450 G/1 LB RED ONIONS,

CUT INTO RINGS

200 ML/7 FL OZ RED WINE

RIND OF 1 ORANGE, GRATED

1 TBSP CASTER SUGAR

SALT AND PEPPER

TO SERVE

BOILED NEW POTATOES

SERVES 4

Preheat the barbecue. To make the marmalade, place the olive oil and onions in a saucepan and sauté gently for 5–10 minutes, until the onions are just softened and beginning to turn golden brown. Add the wine, orange rind and sugar to the saucepan and simmer for 10–15 minutes, until the onions are tender and most of the liquid has evaporated. Leave to cool, then season to taste with salt and pepper.

Make a few cuts in the edge of fat around each steak to prevent the meat curling as it cooks. Using a knife, spread each steak with a little of the mustard and season with salt and pepper.

Mix the sunflower oil, orange juice and rind together in a small bowl, then use to baste the steaks occasionally during cooking.

Cook the steaks over hot coals, searing them over the hottest part of the barbecue for 2 minutes on each side, basting occasionally with the orange juice mixture.

Move the meat to an area with slightly less intense heat and cook, basting occasionally, for 4–10 minutes on each side, depending on how well done you like your steaks. Transfer the steaks to plates and serve with the red onion marmalade and new potatoes.

Alternative Cooking Method

A griddle pan or frying pan can also be used to cook this steak. Ensure that you brush the pan with a little oil first and then pre-heat before adding the meat. Cooking times may be increased slightly as this method of cooking does not generate the high heat of a barbecue. You therefore will need to look for visual signs that the food is cooked to your liking.

2 CHOPS

The perfect choice for midweek meals, chops are wonderfully versatile and this chapter is full of quick and clever ways to make them really special. There are recipes for traditional favourites, such as Minted Lamb Chops (see page 84) and Honey Glazed Pork Chops (see page 108), as well as a range of dishes from countries as diverse as Spain, Greece, Italy, France, the Middle East and the Caribbean. Why not ring the changes with Veal with Pickled Vegetables (see page 76), Persian Lamb Chops (see page 82) or Pork in Lemon Sauce (see page 112) and liven up the family menu?

NEAPOLITAN VEAL CUTLETS
WITH MASCARPONE

200 G/7 OZ BUTTER

4 X 250 G/9 OZ VEAL CUTLETS,
TRIMMED

1 LARGE ONION, SLICED

2 APPLES, PEELED,
CORED AND SLICED

175 G/6 OZ BUTTON MUSHROOMS

1 TBSP CHOPPED FRESH TARRAGON

8 BLACK PEPPERCORNS

1 TBSP SESAME SEEDS

400 G/14 OZ DRIED MARILLE

100 ML/3½ FL OZ EXTRA-VIRGIN
OLIVE OIL

175 G/6 OZ MASCARPONE CHEESE,
BROKEN INTO SMALL PIECES

SALT AND PEPPER

2 LARGE BEEF TOMATOES,
CUT IN HALF

LEAVES OF 1 FRESH BASIL SPRIG

SERVES 4

Melt 60 g/2 oz of the butter in a frying pan. Gently fry the veal for 5 minutes on each side. Transfer to a dish and keep warm.

Fry the onion and apples until golden. Transfer to a dish, top with the veal and keep warm.

Fry the mushrooms, tarragon and peppercorns in the remaining butter for 3 minutes. Sprinkle over the sesame seeds.

Bring a pan of salted water to the boil. Add the pasta and 1 tbsp of the oil and cook until tender. Drain and transfer to a serving plate.

Top the pasta with the cheese and sprinkle over the remaining olive oil. Place the onions, apples and veal cutlets on top of the pasta. Spoon the mushrooms, peppercorns and pan juices on to the cutlets, place the tomatoes and basil leaves around the edge of the plate and place in a preheated oven at 150°C/300°F for 5 minutes. Season to taste with salt and pepper and serve immediately.

LAMB WITH COURGETTES AND TOMATOES

4-8 LAMB CHOPS

PEPPER

2 TBSP OLIVE OIL

1 ONION, CHOPPED FINELY

1 GARLIC CLOVE, CHOPPED FINELY

4 TBSP OUZO (OPTIONAL)

400 G/14 OZ CANNED TOMATOES
IN JUICE

PINCH OF SUGAR

250 G/9 OZ COURGETTES, SLICED

2 TBSP CHOPPED FRESH THYME

SALT

SERVES 4

Season the lamb chops with pepper. Heat the oil in a large, flameproof casserole dish, add the onion and garlic and fry for 5 minutes, until softened. Add the lamb chops and fry until sealed and browned on both sides.

Stir the ouzo into the saucepan, if using, then add the tomatoes with their juice, the sugar, courgettes, thyme and salt. Bring to the boil and then simmer for 30–45 minutes, stirring occasionally and turning the chops once during cooking, until the lamb and courgettes are tender. If necessary, add a little water during cooking if the sauce becomes too thick. Serve hot.

HERBED PORK CHOPS

4 PORK CHOPS

SERVES 4

MARINADE

4 TBSP SUNFLOWER OIL

2 TBSP LEMON JUICE

1 TBSP CHOPPED FRESH
MARJORAM

1 TBSP CHOPPED FRESH THYME

2 TABLESPOONS CHOPPED FRESH
PARSLEY

1 GARLIC CLOVE, FINELY CHOPPED

1 ONION, FINELY CHOPPED

SALT AND PEPPER

BLUE CHEESE AND
WALNUT BUTTER

55 G/2 OZ BUTTER

4 SPRING ONIONS,
FINELY CHOPPED

140 G/5 OZ DOLCELATTE CHEESE,
CRUMBLED

2 TBSP FINELY CHOPPED WALNUTS

TO SERVE

A SMALL SALAD

Trim the fat from the chops and place them in a dish. Whisk together the oil, lemon juice, marjoram, thyme, parsley, garlic and onion in a bowl, then season with salt and pepper. Pour the marinade over the chops, turning to coat. Cover and marinate in the refrigerator overnight.

To make the flavoured butter, melt half the butter in a frying pan and cook the spring onions over a low heat, stirring frequently for a few minutes, until softened. Transfer to a bowl and mix in the remaining butter, the cheese and walnuts. Form into a roll, then cover and chill until required.

Drain the chops, reserving the marinade. Grill the chops on a hot barbecue for 5 minutes on each side, then grill over more medium coals or on a higher rack, turning and brushing occasionally with the reserved marinade, for about 10 minutes more on each side, or until cooked through and tender. Transfer to serving plates and top each chop with 1–2 slices of the cheese and walnut butter. Serve immediately with a small salad.

Alternative Cooking Method

Cook under a hot grill. Cooking times may vary slightly if you use this method so you will need to look for visual signs that the food is cooked to your liking.

LAMB WITH BAY AND
LEMON

4 LAMB CHOPS

1 TBSP SUNFLOWER OIL

15 G/½ OZ BUTTER

150 ML/5 FL OZ WHITE WINE

150 ML/5 FL OZ LAMB OR
VEGETABLE STOCK

2 BAY LEAVES

PARED RIND OF 1 LEMON

SALT AND PEPPER

SERVES 4

Using a sharp knife, carefully remove the bone from each lamb chop, keeping the meat intact. Alternatively, ask the butcher to prepare the lamb noisettes for you.

Shape the meat into rounds and secure with a length of string.

Heat the oil and butter together in a large frying pan until the mixture begins to froth.

Add the lamb noisettes to the frying pan and cook for 2–3 minutes on each side, or until browned all over.

Remove the frying pan from the heat, remove the meat, drain off all of the excess fat and discard. Place the noisettes back in the frying pan.

Return the frying pan to the heat. Add the wine, stock, bay leaves and lemon rind and cook for 20–25 minutes, or until the lamb is tender. Season the lamb and sauce to taste with a little salt and pepper.

Transfer to serving plates. Remove the string from each noisette and serve with the sauce.

VEAL WITH PICKLED VEGETABLES

FOR THE VEGETABLE ESCABECHE

150 ML/¼ PINT OLIVE OIL

4 SHALLOTS, SLICED

2 PINCHES OF SAFFRON THREADS

450 G/1 LB YOUNG CARROTS, PEELED AND SLICED THINLY

225 G/8 OZ FRENCH OR OTHER GREEN BEANS, CHOPPED SMALL

225 G/8 OZ TINY CAULIFLOWER FLORETS

3 TBSP WHITE WINE VINEGAR

1 TSP CORIANDER SEEDS, CRUSHED

½ TSP BLACK PEPPERCORNS, CRUSHED

1 BAY LEAF, TORN IN HALF

4 VEAL LOIN CHOPS, ABOUT 225 G/8 OZ EACH AND 2 CM/¾ INCH THICK

SALT AND PEPPER

TO GARNISH

2 TBSP FINELY SNIPPED FRESH CHIVES

TO SERVE

GARLIC-FLAVOURED OLIVE OIL

SERVES 4

To make the vegetable escabeche, heat the oil in a frying pan over a medium heat. Add the shallots and saffron and fry for 5–7 minutes until the shallots begin to caramelize. Add the carrots, beans and cauliflower. Reduce the heat to very low, cover and cook for 5–8 minutes until the vegetables are tender-crisp. Stir in the vinegar, coriander seeds, peppercorns and bay leaf. Remove from the heat and leave to cool, unless you are serving the dish immediately.

When ready to cook, lightly drizzle the chops with more oil and season with salt and pepper to taste. Place under a preheated hot grill, about 10 cm/4 inches from the source of the heat, and grill for 3 minutes. Turn the chops over and grill for a further 2 minutes if you like them cooked medium.

Transfer the chops to individual plates and spoon a little of the escabeche on the side of each. Sprinkle the vegetables with the chives, and drizzle with a little of the flavoured oil. Serve at once.

BUTTERFLY CHOPS WITH REDCURRANT GLAZE

4 TBSP REDCURRANT JELLY

2 TBSP RASPBERRY VINEGAR

½ TSP DRIED ROSEMARY

1 GARLIC CLOVE, CRUSHED

1 TBSP SUNFLOWER OIL,
PLUS EXTRA FOR BASTING

4 BUTTERFLY LAMB CHOPS OR
8 LOIN LAMB CHOPS

4 BABY AUBERGINES

SERVES 4

Preheat the barbecue. To make the glaze, place the redcurrant jelly, vinegar, rosemary, garlic and sunflower oil in a saucepan and heat, stirring occasionally, until the jelly melts and the ingredients are well blended.

Cook the chops over hot coals for 5 minutes on each side. Cut each aubergine in half and brush the cut sides liberally with sunflower oil. Cook alongside the lamb for 3–4 minutes on each side. Keep warm.

Brush glaze over the chops and barbecue the meat for a further 5 minutes on each side, basting frequently, until the meat is cooked through. Keep the redcurrant glaze warm at the side of the barbecue.

Transfer the lamb and aubergines to warmed serving plates and pour over the remaining redcurrant glaze. Serve immediately.

Alternative Cooking Method

A griddle pan or frying pan can also be used to cook these lamb chops. Ensure that you brush the pan with a little oil first and then pre-heat before adding the meat. Cooking times may be increased slightly as this method of cooking does not generate the high heat of a barbecue. You therefore will need to look for visual signs that the food is cooked to your liking.

GIN AND JUNIPER PORK

4 PORK CHOPS,
ABOUT 175 G/6 OZ EACH

50 ML/2 FL OZ DRY GIN

175 ML/6 FL OZ ORANGE JUICE

2 RED OR WHITE ONIONS,
CUT IN HALF

6 JUNIPER BERRIES,
LIGHTLY CRUSHED

THINLY PARED RIND OF 1 ORANGE

1 CINNAMON STICK

1 BAY LEAF

2 TSP FINELY CHOPPED
FRESH THYME

SALT AND PEPPER

VARIATION

FOR A VARIATION ON THIS
JUNIPER SAUCE,
SEE PAGE 10

SERVES 4

Place the pork chops in a large, shallow, non-metallic dish. Pour in the gin and orange juice and add the onion halves. Add the juniper berries, orange rind, cinnamon stick, bay leaf and thyme and, using a fork, stir well until the pork chops are thoroughly coated. Cover with clingfilm and leave to marinate in the refrigerator for up to 8 hours.

Preheat the barbecue. Drain the pork chops and onions, reserving the marinade. Season the pork chops to taste with salt and pepper and sieve the marinade into a small jug.

Cook the pork and onions over medium hot coals, brushing frequently with the reserved marinade, for 7–9 minutes on each side, or until thoroughly cooked. Transfer to a large serving plate and serve immediately.

Alternative Cooking Method

A griddle pan or frying pan can also be used to cook these chops. Ensure that you brush the pan with a little oil first and then pre-heat before adding the meat. Cooking times may be increased slightly as this method of cooking does not generate the high heat of a barbecue. You therefore will need to look for visual signs that the food is cooked to your liking.

PERSIAN LAMB CHOPS

2 TBSP CHOPPED FRESH MINT

225 ML/8 FL OZ LOW-FAT
NATURAL YOGURT

4 GARLIC CLOVES, CRUSHED

¼ TSP PEPPER

6 LEAN LAMB CHOPS

2 TBSP LEMON JUICE

TABBOULEH

250 G/9 OZ COUSCOUS

500 ML/18 FL OZ BOILING WATER

2 TBSP OLIVE OIL

2 TBSP LEMON JUICE

½ ONION, CHOPPED FINELY

4 TOMATOES, CHOPPED

25 G/1 OZ FRESH CORIANDER,
CHOPPED

2 TBSP CHOPPED FRESH MINT

SALT AND PEPPER

SERVES 4-6

For the marinade, combine the mint, yogurt, garlic and pepper.

Put the chops into a non-porous dish and rub all over with the lemon juice. Pour the marinade over the chops. Cover and marinate for 2–3 hours.

To make the tabbouleh, put the couscous into a heatproof bowl and pour over the boiling water. Leave for 5 minutes. Drain and put into a sieve. Steam over a pan of barely simmering water for 8 minutes. Toss in the oil and lemon juice. Add the onion, tomato and herbs. Season and set aside.

Cook the lamb over a medium barbecue for 15 minutes, turning once. Serve with the tabbouleh.

Alternative Cooking Method

A griddle pan or frying pan can also be used to cook these lamb chops. Ensure that you brush the pan with a little oil first and then pre-heat before adding the meat. Cooking times may be increased slightly as this method of cooking does not generate the high heat of a barbecue. You therefore will need to look for visual signs that the food is cooked to your liking.

MINTED
LAMB CHOPS

6 CHUMP CHOPS,
ABOUT 175 G/6 OZ EACH
150 ML/5 FL OZ NATURAL
GREEK YOGURT
2 GARLIC CLOVES,
FINELY CHOPPED
1 TSP GRATED FRESH
ROOT GINGER
¼ TSP CORIANDER SEEDS,
CRUSHED
SALT AND PEPPER
1 TBSP OLIVE OIL,
PLUS EXTRA FOR BRUSHING
1 TBSP ORANGE JUICE
1 TSP WALNUT OIL
2 TBSP CHOPPED FRESH MINT

SERVES 6

Place the chops in a large, shallow, non-metallic bowl. Mix half the yogurt, the garlic, ginger and coriander seeds together in a jug and season to taste with salt and pepper. Spoon the mixture over the chops, turning to coat, then cover with clingfilm and leave to marinate in the refrigerator for 2 hours, turning occasionally.

Preheat the barbecue. Place the remaining yogurt, the olive oil, orange juice, walnut oil and mint in a small bowl and, using a hand-held whisk, whisk until thoroughly blended. Season to taste with salt and pepper. Cover the minted yogurt with clingfilm and leave to chill in the refrigerator until ready to serve.

Drain the chops, scraping off the marinade. Brush with olive oil and cook over medium hot coals for 5–7 minutes on each side. Serve immediately with the minted yogurt.

Alternative Cooking Method
A griddle pan or frying pan can also be used to cook these chops. Ensure that you brush the pan with a little oil first and then pre-heat before adding the meat. Cooking times may be increased slightly as this method of cooking does not generate the high heat of a barbecue. You therefore will need to look for visual signs that the food is cooked to your liking.

ITALIAN MARINATED PORK CHOPS

4 PORK RIB CHOPS

4 FRESH SAGE LEAVES

2 TBSP SALTED CAPERS

2 GHERKINS, CHOPPED

MARINADE

4 TBSP DRY WHITE WINE

1 TBSP MUSCOVADO SUGAR

2 TBSP OLIVE OIL

1 TSP DIJON MUSTARD

TO GARNISH

A SMALL SALAD

TO SERVE

GARLIC BREAD

VARIATION

FOR A VARIATION ON THIS
WHITE WINE MARINADE,
SEE PAGE 10

SERVES 4

Trim any visible fat from the chops and place them in a large, shallow dish. Top each with a sage leaf. Rub the salt off the capers with your fingers and sprinkle them over the chops, together with the gherkins.

Mix the wine, sugar, oil and mustard together in a small bowl and pour the mixture over the chops. Cover with clingfilm and marinate in a cool place for about 2 hours.

Drain the chops, reserving the marinade. Grill the chops on a hot barbecue for 5 minutes on each side, then grill over more medium coals or on a higher rack, turning and brushing occasionally with the reserved marinade, for about 10 minutes more on each side, or until cooked through and tender. Serve immediately with a small salad and garlic bread if you like.

Alternative Cooking Method

A griddle pan or frying pan can also be used to cook these chops. Ensure that you brush the pan with a little oil first and then pre-heat before adding the meat. Cooking times may be increased slightly as this method of cooking does not generate the high heat of a barbecue. You therefore will need to look for visual signs that the food is cooked to your liking.

ROAST TOMATO AND LAMB PARCELS

1 TBSP VEGETABLE OIL

1 LARGE LAMB CHOP OR STEAK

4 CHERRY TOMATOES

1 GARLIC CLOVE, CRUSHED

2 TSP FRESH TORN OREGANO OR

CHOPPED ROSEMARY

SALT AND PEPPER

SERVES 1

Preheat the oven to 160°C/325°F/Gas Mark 3.

Heat the oil over a high heat in a heavy frying pan and brown the lamb chop on both sides.

Cut a large square of tin foil. Drain the meat and place in the centre of the foil. Arrange the tomatoes and garlic on top of the meat. Sprinkle with the torn oregano or chopped rosemary, salt and pepper. Fold the foil to seal the parcel and transfer to a baking tray.

Bake in the oven for 45 minutes, or until the meat is tender.

Open the parcel carefully so that the steam can escape, then transfer the meat and tomatoes to a serving dish. Spoon over the juices from the meat.

STICKY PORK CHOPS

SAUCE

50 ML/2 FL OZ PLUM, HOISIN,
SWEET & SOUR OR DUCK SAUCE

1 TSP DARK BROWN SUGAR

1 TBSP TOMATO KETCHUP

PINCH OF GARLIC POWDER

2 TBSP DARK SOY SAUCE

4 LEAN PORK CHOPS (OR STEAKS)

TO SERVE

COOKED RICE AND PEAS

SERVES 4

Preheat the griddle over a high heat.

Combine the sauce, brown sugar, ketchup, garlic powder and soy sauce in a small mixing bowl.

Arrange the pork chops in a single layer on a flat dish. Brush the tops with sauce, then place the chops, sauce side down, on the griddle. Cook the chops for 5 minutes, pressing down occasionally to get dark grid marks.

Brush the upper side of the chops with sauce, turn and continue cooking for 5 minutes, or until dark grid marks appear.

Reduce the heat to medium and, turning once, cook the chops for about 10 more minutes, or until they are firm and the juices run clear when pierced with a skewer.

Transfer the chops to a large dish and serve immediately, with the peas and rice.

LAMB WITH AUBERGINE

1 AUBERGINE

SALT AND PEPPER

4-8 LAMB CHOPS

3 TBSP OLIVE OIL

1 ONION, CHOPPED ROUGHLY

1 GARLIC CLOVE, CHOPPED FINELY

400 G/14 OZ CANNED CHOPPED

TOMATOES IN JUICE

PINCH OF SUGAR

16 BLACK OLIVES, STONED AND

CHOPPED ROUGHLY

1 TSP CHOPPED FRESH HERBS

SUCH AS BASIL, FLAT-LEAF

PARSLEY OR OREGANO

SERVES 4

Cut the aubergine into 2-cm/¾-inch cubes, put in a colander, standing over a large plate, and sprinkle each layer with salt. Cover with a plate and place a heavy weight on top. Leave for 30 minutes to degorge.

Preheat the grill. Rinse the aubergine slices under cold running water, then pat dry with kitchen paper. Season the lamb chops with pepper.

Place the lamb chops on the grill pan and cook under a medium heat for 10-15 minutes until tender, turning once during the cooking time.

Meanwhile, heat the olive oil in a saucepan, add the aubergine, onion and garlic and fry for 10 minutes, until softened and starting to brown. Add the tomatoes and their juice, the sugar, olives, chopped herbs, salt and pepper and simmer for 5-10 minutes.

To serve, spoon the sauce onto 4 warmed serving plates and top with the lamb chops.

CARIBBEAN PORK

4 PORK LOIN CHOPS

4 TBSP DARK MUSCOVADO SUGAR

4 TBSP ORANGE OR
PINEAPPLE JUICE

2 TBSP JAMAICAN RUM

1 TBSP DESICCATED COCONUT

½ TSP GROUND CINNAMON

COCONUT RICE

225 G/8 OZ BASMATI RICE

450 ML/16 FL OZ WATER

150 ML/5 FL OZ COCONUT MILK

4 TBSP RAISINS

4 TBSP ROASTED PEANUTS OR
CASHEW NUTS

SALT AND PEPPER

2 TBSP DESICCATED COCONUT,
TOASTED

TO SERVE

MIXED SALAD LEAVES

SERVES 4

Trim any excess fat from the pork and place the chops in a shallow, non-metallic dish. Mix the sugar, fruit juice, rum, coconut and cinnamon together in a bowl, stirring until the sugar dissolves. Pour the mixture over the pork, cover and leave to marinate in the refrigerator for at least 2 hours, or preferably overnight.

Preheat the barbecue. Remove the pork from the marinade, reserving the liquid for basting. Cook over hot coals for 15–20 minutes, basting with the marinade.

Meanwhile, make the coconut rice. Rinse the rice under cold running water, place it in a saucepan with the water and coconut milk and bring gently to the boil. Stir, cover and reduce the heat. Simmer gently for 12 minutes, or until the rice is tender and the liquid has been absorbed. Fluff up with a fork.

Stir the raisins and nuts into the rice, season to taste with salt and pepper and sprinkle with the coconut. Transfer the pork and rice to warmed serving plates and serve immediately with mixed salad leaves.

Alternative Cooking Method

A griddle pan or frying pan can also be used to cook these pork chops. Ensure that you brush the pan with a little oil first and then pre-heat before adding the meat. Cooking times may be increased slightly as this method of cooking does not generate the high heat of a barbecue. You therefore will need to look for visual signs that the food is cooked to your liking.

SOZZLED LAMB CHOPS

8 LAMB LOIN CHOPS

MARINADE

2 TBSP EXTRA-VIRGIN OLIVE OIL
2 TBSP WORCESTERSHIRE SAUCE
2 TBSP LEMON JUICE
2 TBSP DRY GIN
1 GARLIC CLOVE, FINELY CHOPPED
SALT AND PEPPER

MUSTARD BUTTER

55 G/2 OZ UNSALTED BUTTER,
SOFTENED
1½ TSP TARRAGON MUSTARD
1 TBSP CHOPPED FRESH PARSLEY
DASH OF LEMON JUICE

TO GARNISH

FRESH PARSLEY SPRIGS

TO SERVE

SALAD

SERVES 4

Preheat the barbecue. Place the lamb chops in a large, shallow, non-metallic dish. Mix all the ingredients for the marinade together in a jug, seasoning to taste with salt and pepper. Pour the mixture over the chops and then turn them until they are thoroughly coated. Cover with clingfilm and leave to marinate for 5 minutes.

To make the mustard butter, mix all the ingredients together in a small bowl, beating with a fork until well blended. Cover with clingfilm and leave to chill in the refrigerator until required.

Drain the chops, reserving the marinade. Cook over medium hot coals, brushing frequently with the reserved marinade, for 5 minutes on each side. Transfer to serving plates, top with the mustard butter and garnish with parsley sprigs. Serve immediately with salad.

Alternative Cooking Method

A griddle pan or frying pan can also be used to cook these chops. Ensure that you brush the pan with a little oil first and then pre-heat before adding the meat. Cooking times may be increased slightly as this method of cooking does not generate the high heat of a barbecue. You therefore will need to look for visual signs that the food is cooked to your liking.

VIRGINIAN
PORK CHOPS

2 TBSP SUNFLOWER OIL

4 PORK CHOPS,
ABOUT 175 G/6 OZ EACH

2 TBSP WHITE WINE

1 ONION, CHOPPED

415 G/14½ OZ CANNED PEACH
HALVES IN NATURAL JUICE,
DRAINED

1 TBSP PINK OR GREEN
PEPPERCORNS

150 ML/5 FL OZ CHICKEN STOCK

2–3 TSP BALSAMIC VINEGAR

SALT AND PEPPER

SERVES 4

Heat half the sunflower oil in a large, heavy-based frying pan. Add the chops and cook for 6 minutes on each side, or until browned and cooked through. Transfer to a plate, cover and keep warm. Pour off any excess fat from the frying pan and return to the heat. Add the wine and cook, for 2 minutes, stirring and scraping up any sediment from the base of the frying pan. Pour the liquid over the meat, re-cover and keep warm.

Wipe out the frying pan with kitchen paper and heat the remaining sunflower oil. Add the onion and cook over a low heat, stirring occasionally, for 5 minutes, or until softened. Meanwhile, slice the peach halves.

Add the peaches to the frying pan and heat through for 1 minute. Stir in the peppercorns, pour in the chicken stock and bring to simmering point. Return the chops and cooking juices to the frying pan and season to taste with vinegar, salt and pepper. Transfer to warmed plates and serve.

ITALIAN
LAMB CHOPS

4 LAMB CHOPS OR 8 LAMB CUTLETS

4 TOMATOES, HALVED

SERVES 4

MARINADE

2 TSP DRIED OREGANO

JUICE OF ½ LEMON

2 TBSP EXTRA-VIRGIN OLIVE OIL

TO GARNISH

A FEW BASIL LEAVES

TO SERVE

COOKED LINGUINE OR
OTHER PASTA

Arrange the lamb in a single layer in a shallow dish. Sprinkle with oregano, lemon juice and oil. Cover the dish with clingfilm and refrigerate overnight or for as long as possible.

About 10 minutes before cooking, remove the lamb from the refrigerator. Meanwhile, preheat the griddle over a high heat.

Place the lamb on the griddle and sear for 2 minutes on each side. Reduce the heat and cook over a medium heat for about 5 minutes longer, turning the pieces over once. If the chops are thick, you may need to allow a few extra minutes. The meat is best when it is pink inside.

Two to three minutes before the meat is ready, cook the tomato pieces on the griddle. Arrange the chops and cooked tomatoes on a large platter and serve immediately with the pasta, garnished with basil leaves.

PORK CHOPS WITH SAGE

2 TBSP FLOUR

1 TBSP CHOPPED FRESH SAGE OR

1 TSP DRIED

4 LEAN BONELESS PORK CHOPS,

TRIMMED OF EXCESS FAT

2 TBSP OLIVE OIL

15 G/½ OZ BUTTER

2 RED ONIONS, SLICED INTO RINGS

1 TBSP LEMON JUICE

2 TSP CASTER SUGAR

4 PLUM TOMATOES, QUARTERED

SALT AND PEPPER

TO SERVE

A GREEN SALAD

SERVES 4

Mix the flour, sage and salt and pepper to taste on a plate. Lightly dust the pork chops on both sides with the seasoned flour.

Heat the oil and butter in a frying pan, add the chops and cook them for 6–7 minutes on each side until cooked through. Drain the chops, reserving the pan juices, and keep warm.

Toss the onion in the lemon juice and fry along with the sugar and tomatoes for 5 minutes until tender.

Serve the pork with the tomato and onion mixture and a green salad.

GRIDDLED PORK WITH ORANGE SAUCE

4 TBSP FRESHLY SQUEEZED
ORANGE JUICE

4 TBSP RED WINE VINEGAR

2 GARLIC CLOVES,
FINELY CHOPPED

PEPPER

4 PORK STEAKS,
TRIMMED OF ALL VISIBLE FAT

OLIVE OIL, FOR BRUSHING

GREMOLATA

3 TBSP FINELY CHOPPED
FRESH PARSLEY

GRATED RIND OF 1 LIME

GRATED RIND OF ½ LEMON

1 GARLIC CLOVE,
VERY FINELY CHOPPED

SERVES 4

Mix the orange juice, vinegar and garlic together in a shallow, non-metallic dish and season to taste with pepper. Add the pork, turning to coat. Cover and leave in the refrigerator to marinate for up to 3 hours.

Meanwhile, mix all the Gremolata ingredients together in a small mixing bowl, cover with clingfilm and leave to chill in the refrigerator until required.

Heat a non-stick griddle pan and brush lightly with olive oil. Remove the pork from the marinade, reserving the marinade, add to the pan and cook over a medium–high heat for 5 minutes on each side, or until the juices run clear when the meat is pierced with a skewer.

Meanwhile, pour the marinade into a small saucepan and simmer over a medium heat for 5 minutes, or until slightly thickened. Transfer the pork to a serving dish, pour the orange sauce over it and sprinkle with the Gremolata. Serve immediately.

PORK WITH FENNEL
AND JUNIPER

½ FENNEL BULB

1 TBSP JUNIPER BERRIES

ABOUT 2 TBSP OLIVE OIL

FINELY GRATED RIND AND

JUICE OF 1 ORANGE

4 PORK CHOPS,

EACH ABOUT 150 G/5½ OZ

TO SERVE

FRESH BREAD AND

A CRISP SALAD

VARIATION

FOR A VARIATION ON THIS

JUNIPER SAUCE,

SEE PAGE 10

SERVES 4

Finely chop the fennel bulb, discarding the green parts.

Grind the juniper berries in a pestle and mortar. Mix the crushed juniper berries with the fennel flesh, olive oil and orange rind.

Using a sharp knife, score a few cuts all over each chop.

Place the pork chops in a roasting tin or an ovenproof dish. Spoon the fennel and juniper mixture over the chops.

Pour the orange juice over the top of each chop, cover and marinate in the refrigerator for about 2 hours.

Cook the pork chops, under a preheated grill, for 10–15 minutes, depending on the thickness of the meat, or until the meat is tender and cooked through, turning occasionally.

Transfer the pork chops to serving plates and serve with a crisp, fresh salad and plenty of fresh bread to mop up the cooking juices.

HONEY-GLAZED
PORK CHOPS

4 LEAN PORK LOIN CHOPS

SALT AND PEPPER

4 TBSP CLEAR HONEY

1 TBSP DRY SHERRY

4 TBSP ORANGE JUICE

2 TBSP OLIVE OIL

2.5-CM/1-INCH PIECE FRESH ROOT
GINGER, GRATED

SUNFLOWER OIL, FOR OILING

SERVES 4

Preheat the barbecue. Season the pork chops with salt and pepper to taste. Reserve while you make the glaze.

To make the glaze, place the honey, sherry, orange juice, olive oil and ginger in a small saucepan and heat gently, stirring constantly, until well blended.

Cook the pork chops on an oiled rack over hot coals for 5 minutes on each side.

Brush the chops with the glaze and barbecue for a further 2–4 minutes on each side, basting frequently with the glaze.

Transfer the pork chops to warmed serving plates and serve hot.

Alternative Cooking Method

A griddle pan or frying pan can also be used to cook these pork chops. Ensure that you brush the pan with a little oil first and then pre-heat before adding the meat. Cooking times may be increased slightly as this method of cooking does not generate the high heat of a barbecue. You therefore will need to look for visual signs that the food is cooked to your liking.

LAMB CUTLETS WITH ROSEMARY

8 LAMB CUTLETS

5 TBSP OLIVE OIL

2 TBSP LEMON JUICE

1 GARLIC CLOVE, CRUSHED

½ TSP LEMON PEPPER

SALT

8 FRESH ROSEMARY SPRIGS

SALAD

4 TOMATOES, SLICED

4 SPRING ONIONS,
DIAGONALLY SLICED

DRESSING

2 TBSP OLIVE OIL

1 TBSP LEMON JUICE

1 GARLIC CLOVE, CHOPPED

¼ TSP FINELY CHOPPED FRESH
ROSEMARY

SERVES 4

Preheat the barbecue. Trim the lamb by cutting away the flesh to expose the tips of the bones.

Place the oil, lemon juice, garlic, lemon, pepper and salt in a shallow non-metallic dish and whisk with a fork to combine.

Lay the rosemary sprigs in the dish and place the lamb on top. Cover and leave to marinate for at least 1 hour, turning the lamb cutlets once.

Remove the chops from the marinade and wrap foil around the exposed bones to stop them from burning.

Place the rosemary sprigs on the rack and place the lamb on top. Barbecue over hot coals for 10–15 minutes, turning once.

Meanwhile, make the salad and dressing. Arrange the tomatoes on a serving dish and sprinkle the spring onions on top. Place all the ingredients for the dressing in a screw-top jar, shake well and pour over the salad. Serve with the barbecued lamb cutlets.

Alternative Cooking Method

A griddle pan or frying pan can also be used to cook these lamb cutlets. Ensure that you brush the pan with a little oil first and then pre-heat before adding the meat. Cooking times may be increased slightly as this method of cooking does not generate the high heat of a barbecue. You therefore will need to look for visual signs that the food is cooked to your liking.

PORK IN LEMON SAUCE

4 PORK CHOPS (OR LOIN STEAKS)

PEPPER

2 TBSP OLIVE OIL

BUNCH SPRING ONIONS,
WHITE PARTS ONLY, SLICED THINLY

1 COS LETTUCE,
SLICED THINLY WIDTHWAYS

1 TBSP CHOPPED FRESH DILL

225 ML/8 FL OZ CHICKEN STOCK

2 EGGS

JUICE OF 1 LARGE LEMON

SALT

SERVES 4

Season the pork chops with pepper. Heat the oil in a large, heavy-based frying pan, add the spring onions and fry for 2 minutes until softened. Add the pork chops and fry for 10 minutes, turning the chops several times, until browned on both sides and tender.

When the pork chops are cooked, add the lettuce, dill and stock to the frying pan. Bring to the boil, cover and then simmer for 4-5 minutes, until the lettuce has wilted.

Meanwhile, put the eggs and lemon juice in a large bowl and whisk together.

When the lettuce has wilted remove the pork chops and lettuce from the frying pan with a slotted spoon, put in a warmed serving dish and keep warm in a low oven. Strain the cooking liquid into a jug.

Gradually add 4 tbsp of the hot cooking liquid to the lemon mixture, whisking all the time. Pour the egg mixture into the frying pan and simmer for 2-3 minutes, whisking all the time, until the sauce thickens. (Do not boil or the sauce will curdle.) Season with salt and pepper. Pour the sauce over the pork chops and lettuce and serve hot.

PORK CHOPS AND
SPICY BEANS

3 TBSP VEGETABLE OIL

4 LEAN PORK CHOPS,
RIND REMOVED

2 ONIONS, PEELED AND
THINLY SLICED

2 GARLIC CLOVES,
PEELED AND CRUSHED

2 FRESH GREEN CHILLIES,
SEEDED AND CHOPPED OR USE
1-2 TSP MINCED CHILLI

2.5 CM/1 IN PIECE GINGER ROOT,
PEELED AND CHOPPED

1½ TSP CUMIN SEEDS

1½ TSP GROUND CORIANDER

600 ML/1 PINT STOCK OR WATER

2 TBSP TOMATO PURÉE

½ AUBERGINE, TRIMMED AND
CUT INTO 1 CM/½ INCH DICE

SALT

1 X 400 G/14 OZ CAN RED KIDNEY
BEANS, DRAINED

4 TBSP DOUBLE CREAM

TO GARNISH

SPRIGS OF CORIANDER

SERVES 4

Heat the vegetable oil in a large frying pan, add the pork chops and fry until sealed and browned on both sides. Remove from the pan and set aside until required.

Add the sliced onions, garlic, chillies, ginger and spices and fry gently for 2 minutes. Stir in the stock or water, tomato purée, diced aubergine and season with salt and pepper.

Bring the mixture to the boil, place the pork chops on top, then cover and simmer gently over medium heat for 30 minutes.

Remove the chops for a moment and stir the red kidney beans and double cream into the mixture. Return the chops to the pan, cover and heat through gently for 5 minutes.

Taste and adjust the seasoning, if necessary. Serve hot, garnished with coriander sprigs.

VEAL CHOPS WITH WILD
MUSHROOM SAUCE

4 VEAL LOIN CHOPS,
2 CM/¾ INCH THICK
GARLIC- OR PAPRIKA-FLAVOURED
OLIVE OIL
SALT AND PEPPER

FOR THE WILD MUSHROOM SAUCE
300 ML/10 FL OZ MADEIRA
55 G/2 OZ BUTTER
2 SHALLOTS, FINELY CHOPPED
500 G/1 LB 2 OZ MIXED WILD
MUSHROOMS, SUCH AS CEPS,
CHANTERELLES, MORELS AND
SHIITAKES, WIPED, TRIMMED
AND SLICED IF LARGE
500 ML/18 FL OZ VEGETABLE
STOCK
FRESHLY GRATED NUTMEG
SALT AND PEPPER

SERVES 4

To make the Wild Mushroom Sauce, put the Madeira in a small saucepan over a high heat and boil until it reduces by half, then set aside. Melt the butter in a large sauté or frying pan over a medium-high heat. Add the shallots and sauté for 2–3 minutes, or until soft, but not brown.

Stir the mushrooms into the pan and continue sautéeing until they give off their liquid. Pour in the stock and bring to the boil, stirring. Reduce the heat to low and leave the stock to simmer until it reduces by half. Stir in the reduced Madeira and continue simmering until only about 6 tablespoons of the liquid are left. Add a few gratings of nutmeg, then season to taste with salt and pepper.

Meanwhile, preheat the grill to high. Lightly brush the veal chops with the oil and season to taste with salt and pepper. Transfer to the grill rack. Grill the veal chops for 3 minutes. Turn them over, brush again with the oil and season to taste with salt and pepper. Continue grilling for a further 3–4 minutes until tender and cooked as desired. Transfer the chops to serving plates and spoon the Wild Mushroom Sauce alongside.

VEAL CHOPS WITH SALSA VERDE

4 VEAL CHOPS, SUCH AS LOIN
CHOPS, ABOUT 225 G/8 OZ EACH
AND 2 CM/¾ INCH THICK
GARLIC-FLAVOURED OLIVE OIL,
FOR BRUSHING
SALT AND PEPPER

SALSA VERDE

60 G/2 OZ FRESH FLAT-LEAF
PARSLEY LEAVES
3 CANNED ANCHOVY FILLETS IN
OIL, DRAINED
½ TBSP CAPERS IN BRINE,
RINSED AND DRAINED
1 SHALLOT, FINELY CHOPPED
1 GARLIC CLOVE, HALVED, GREEN
CORE REMOVED AND CHOPPED
1 TBSP LEMON JUICE, OR TO TASTE
6 LARGE FRESH BASIL LEAVES
2 SPRIGS FRESH OREGANO
120 ML/4 FL OZ/½ CUP EXTRA-
VIRGIN OLIVE OIL

TO GARNISH
FRESH BASIL OR
OREGANO LEAVES

SERVES 4

To make the salsa verde, put all the ingredients, except the olive oil, in a blender or food processor and process until they are chopped and blended.

With the motor running, add the oil through the top or feed tube and quickly blend until thickened. Add pepper to taste. Transfer to a bowl, cover and chill.

Lightly brush the veal chops with olive oil and season them with salt and pepper. Place under a preheated grill and cook for about 3 minutes. Turn over, brush with more oil and grill for a further 2 minutes until cooked when tested with the tip of a knife.

Transfer the chops to individual plates and spoon a little of the chilled salsa verde alongside them. Garnish the chops with fresh oregano or basil and serve with the remaining salsa verde handed separately.

3 ROASTS

Roasts are much easier to cook than many people think and are ideal for family gatherings and entertaining guests. They look impressive, smell appetizing, taste wonderful and the choice of different meats, particular cuts and methods of preparation is huge. Whether your taste is for the traditional, such as Roast Pork with Crackling (see page 134), the sophisticated, such as Festive Beef Wellington (see page 160), the exotic, such as Red Roast Pork in Soy Sauce (see page 146) or the unusual, such as Cypriot Lamb with Orzo (see page 148), you are sure to find the perfect recipe for any occasion.

ROAST LOIN OF PORK

1 KG/2 LB 4 OZ PIECE OF PORK LOIN,
CHINED (BACKBONE REMOVED)
AND THE RIND SCORED BY
THE BUTCHER
1 TBSP FLOUR
300 ML/10 FL OZ DRY CIDER,
APPLE JUICE, CHICKEN STOCK OR
VEGETABLE STOCK

STUFFING

1 TBSP MELTED BUTTER
½ ONION, PEELED AND
FINELY CHOPPED
1 GARLIC CLOVE, PEELED AND
FINELY CHOPPED
1 CM/½ INCH ROOT GINGER,
PEELED AND FINELY CHOPPED
1 PEAR, CORED AND CHOPPED
6 FRESH SAGE LEAVES, CHOPPED
55 G/2 OZ FRESH BREADCRUMBS,
WHITE OR WHOLEMEAL
SALT AND PEPPER

TO SERVE

ROAST POTATOES AND
COOKED SEASONAL VEGETABLES

SERVES 4

Preheat the oven to 220ºC/425ºF/Gas 7. Make the stuffing by heating the butter in a small saucepan and frying the onion and garlic over a medium heat for 3 minutes until soft. Add the ginger and pear, mix well and cook for a further minute.

Remove from the heat and stir in the sage and breadcrumbs, and season well.

Put the stuffing in the joint along the middle of the loin, then roll it up and tie with string; you will need 4–5 pieces to hold the joint in shape. You can cover the stuffing on the ends with small pieces of foil to stop it burning.

Season well, and in particular use a lot of salt on the rind to make a crisp crackling. Place the joint in a roasting tin and roast in the centre of the preheated oven for 20 minutes.

Reduce the heat to 180°C/350°F/Gas 4 and cook for an hour until the skin is crispy and the juices run clear when the joint is pierced with a skewer.

Remove from the oven, lift out the meat and place on a hot serving plate. Cover with foil and leave in a warm place.

Pour off most of the fat from the roasting tin, leaving the meat juices and sediments behind. Sprinkle in the flour and whisk well. Cook the paste for a couple of minutes, then add the cider, apple juice or stock a little at a time until you have a smooth gravy. Boil for 2–3 minutes until the gravy is the required consistency. Season well and pour into a hot serving jug.

Cut the string from the joint and remove the crackling by cutting into the fat. Carve the stuffed pork into slices and serve on hot plates with pieces of crackling and the gravy. Serve with roast potatoes and cooked vegetables in season.

STUFFED SHOULDER OF LAMB

1.8 KG/4 LB SHOULDER OF
LAMB, BONED

SALT AND PEPPER

STUFFING

1 TBSP BUTTER, MELTED

1 ONION, PEELED AND
FINELY CHOPPED

1 GARLIC CLOVE, PEELED AND
FINELY CHOPPED

115 G/4 OZ MINCED VEAL OR PORK

115 G/4 OZ FRESH BREADCRUMBS,
WHITE OR WHOLEMEAL

GRATED ZEST AND JUICE OF
1 LEMON

1 TBSP CHOPPED FRESH PARSLEY

1 TBSP CHOPPED FRESH ROSEMARY

1 TBSP OLIVE OIL

225 ML/8 FL OZ RED WINE

TO SERVE

FLAGEOLET BEANS, COOKED WITH
A CRUSHED CLOVE OF GARLIC AND
1 TBSP CHOPPED FRESH PARSLEY

SERVES 6-8

Preheat the oven to 200°C/400°F/Gas 6. Wipe the lamb with kitchen paper and season well inside and out. To make the stuffing, melt the butter in a small saucepan and fry the onion and garlic over a medium heat for about 3 minutes until soft and transparent. Transfer to a large bowl and mix with the veal, breadcrumbs, lemon juice and zest, and herbs.

Season the mixture well. Using your hands, carefully put the stuffing into the shoulder.

Sew up the pocket to form a good shape (do not worry about the stitches – they will be removed – but try to use only one piece of string).

Place the lamb in a roasting tin and rub over with the oil. Season with salt and pepper, and roast in the centre of the preheated oven for 1½ hours, basting from time to time.

Remove the tin from the oven, then lift out the meat and place on a warm serving plate. Remove all the string, cover the meat with foil and keep it warm.

Pour off the excess fat from the tin and make a simple gravy with the remaining juices. Add the red wine, scrape all the sediment off the bottom of the tin and boil vigorously for 2–3 minutes until well reduced. Pour the gravy into a warm jug. Serve the lamb thickly sliced with flageolet beans, simply heated with a crushed clove of garlic and a tablespoon of chopped parsley.

SLOW-ROASTED
PORK

1.6 KG/3 LB 8 OZ LOIN OF PORK,
BONED AND ROLLED

4 GARLIC CLOVES,
SLICED THINLY LENGTHWAYS

1½ TSP FINELY CHOPPED FRESH
FENNEL FRONDS OR
½ TSP DRIED FENNEL

4 CLOVES

SALT AND PEPPER

300 ML/½ PINT DRY WHITE WINE

300 ML/½ PINT WATER

SERVES 6

Use a small, sharp knife to make incisions all over the pork, opening them out slightly to make little pockets. Place the garlic slices in a small sieve and rinse under cold running water to moisten. Spread out the fennel on a saucer and roll the garlic slices in it to coat. Slide the garlic slices and the cloves into the pockets in the pork. Season the meat all over with salt and pepper.

Place the pork in a large ovenproof dish or roasting tin. Pour in the wine and water. Cook in a preheated oven, 150°C/300°F/ Gas Mark 2, basting the meat occasionally, for 2½–2¾ hours, until the pork is tender but still quite moist.

If you are serving the pork hot, transfer it to a carving board and cut into slices. If you are serving it cold, leave it to cool completely in the cooking juices before removing and slicing.

STUFFED PORK FILLET

2 PORK FILLETS,
ABOUT 500 G/1 LB 2 OZ EACH,
TRIMMED OF ALL VISIBLE FAT

STUFFING

2 RED ONIONS, FINELY CHOPPED

115 G/4 OZ FRESH WHOLEMEAL
BREADCRUMBS

85 G/3 OZ NO-SOAK DRIED
PRUNES, CHOPPED

85 G/3 OZ NO-SOAK DRIED
APRICOTS, CHOPPED

PINCH OF GRATED NUTMEG

PINCH OF GROUND CINNAMON

SALT AND PEPPER

1 EGG WHITE, LIGHTLY BEATEN

SERVES 8

Preheat the oven to 200°C/400°F/Gas Mark 6. To make the stuffing, mix the onions, breadcrumbs, prunes and apricots together. Season to taste with nutmeg, cinnamon, and salt and pepper. Stir in the egg white.

Cut a 13-cm/5-inch long piece from the narrow end of each pork fillet, then cut all the pieces almost completely in half lengthways and open them out. Spread half the filling evenly over one of the longer pieces, then cover with both the smaller pieces, overlapping the narrow ends slightly. Spread the remaining filling on top and cover with the remaining piece of pork. Tie the pork loaf together with kitchen string or trussing thread at intervals along its length. Wrap it securely in foil and place in a roasting tin.

Cook the pork in the preheated oven for 1½ hours. If serving hot, leave to stand for 10 minutes before unwrapping, cutting off the string and slicing. If serving cold, leave to cool in the wrapping, then leave to chill in the refrigerator for at least 2 hours and up to 6 hours before unwrapping and slicing.

CHA SIU

675 G/1½ LB PORK LOIN

3 TBSP HONEY, DISSOLVED IN
1 TBSP BOILING WATER

FOR THE MARINADE

1 TBSP YELLOW BEAN SAUCE,
LIGHTLY CRUSHED

1 TBSP RED FERMENTED BEANCURD

1 TBSP HOISIN SAUCE

1 TBSP OYSTER SAUCE

1 TBSP DARK SOY SAUCE

1 TBSP SUGAR

2 TBSP SHAOXING RICE WINE

1 TSP SESAME OIL

SERVES 4-6

Combine all the marinade ingredients together. Cut the pork loin lengthways into 2 pieces. Arrange in a single layer in a dish and pour the marinade over the top. Cover and leave to marinate for at least 2 hours, basting occasionally.

Preheat the oven to 220°C/425°F/Gas Mark 7. On a wire cooling rack, lay out the pieces of pork in a single layer, reserving the marinade. Place the rack over a dish of boiling water and bake for about 15 minutes, ensuring that there is always a little water in the pan.

Reduce the oven temperature to 180°C/350°F/Gas Mark 4. Turn the strips over and baste with the marinade. Cook for a further 10 minutes.

Remove from the oven and preheat the grill. Brush the pork with the honey and place under the grill for a few minutes, turning once. Cool and use as required, cut into chunks, thin slices or tiny cubes.

PORK STUFFED WITH PROSCIUTTO

500 G/1 LB 2 OZ PIECE OF LEAN
PORK FILLET
SMALL BUNCH FRESH OF BASIL
LEAVES, WASHED
2 TBSP FRESHLY GRATED
PARMESAN
2 TBSP SUN-DRIED TOMATO PASTE
6 THIN SLICES PARMA HAM
1 TBSP OLIVE OIL
SALT AND PEPPER

OLIVE PASTE
125 G/4½ OZ PITTED BLACK OLIVES
4 TBSP OLIVE OIL
2 GARLIC CLOVES, PEELED

SERVES 4

Trim away excess fat and membrane from the pork fillet. Slice the pork lengthways down the middle, taking care not to cut all the way through.

Open out the pork and season the inside. Lay the basil leaves down the centre. Mix the cheese and sun-dried tomato paste and spread over the basil.

Press the pork back together. Wrap the ham around the pork, overlapping, to cover. Place on a rack in a roasting tin, seamside down, and brush with oil. Bake in a preheated oven, 190°C/375°F/Gas Mark 5, for 30–40 minutes depending on thickness until cooked through. Allow to stand for 10 minutes.

For the olive paste, place all the ingredients in a blender or food processor and blend until smooth. Alternatively, for a coarser paste, finely chop the olives and garlic and mix with the oil.

Drain the cooked pork and slice thinly. Serve with the olive paste and a salad.

ROAST PORK WITH CRACKLING

1 KG/2 LB 4 OZ PIECE OF PORK LOIN, BONED AND THE SKIN REMOVED AND RESERVED
SALT AND PEPPER
2 TBSP MUSTARD

FOR THE GRAVY
1 TBSP FLOUR
300 ML/10 FL OZ CIDER, APPLE JUICE OR STOCK

APPLE SAUCE
PEEL, CORE AND SLICE 450 G/1 LB BRAMLEY APPLES INTO A MEDIUM SAUCEPAN. ADD 3 TABLESPOONS WATER AND 15 G/½ OZ CASTER SUGAR AND COOK OVER A GENTLE HEAT FOR 10 MINUTES, STIRRING FROM TIME TO TIME. A LITTLE GROUND CINNAMON COULD BE ADDED, AS COULD 15 G/½ OZ BUTTER, IF DESIRED. BEAT WELL UNTIL THE SAUCE IS THICK AND SMOOTH – USE A HAND MIXER FOR A REALLY SMOOTH FINISH.

TO SERVE
APPLE SAUCE

SERVES 4

Preheat the oven to 200°C/400°F/Gas Mark 6.

Make sure the skin of the pork is well scored and sprinkle with the salt. Place on a wire rack on a baking tray and roast for 30–40 minutes until the crackling is golden brown and crispy.

Season the loin of pork well with salt and pepper and spread the fat with the mustard. Place in a roasting tin and roast in the centre of the oven for 20 minutes. Reduce the oven temperature to 190°C/375°F/Gas Mark 5 and cook for 50–60 minutes until the meat is a good colour and the juices run clear when pierced with a skewer.

Remove the meat from the oven and place on a hot serving plate, cover with foil and leave in a warm place.

To make the gravy, pour off most of the fat from the roasting tin, leaving the meat juices and the sediments. Sprinkle in the flour, whisking well. Cook the paste for a couple of minutes, then add the cider a little at a time until you have a smooth gravy. Boil for 2–3 minutes until it is the required consistency. Season well with salt and pepper and pour into a hot serving jug.

Carve the pork into slices and serve on hot plates with pieces of the crackling and the gravy. Accompany with apple sauce.

VITELLO TONNATO

1 BONED AND ROLLED PIECE OF
VEAL LEG, ABOUT 900 G/2 LB
BONED WEIGHT
OLIVE OIL
SALT AND PEPPER

TUNA MAYONNAISE

150 G/5½ OZ CAN TUNA IN OLIVE OIL
2 LARGE EGGS
ABOUT 3 TBSP LEMON JUICE
OLIVE OIL

8 BLACK OLIVES,
STONED AND HALVED
1 TBSP CAPERS IN BRINE,
RINSED AND DRAINED
FINELY CHOPPED FRESH
FLAT-LEAF PARSLEY

TO GARNISH
LEMON WEDGES

SERVES 6-8

Rub the veal all over with oil and pepper and place in a roasting tin. Cover the meat with a piece of foil if there isn't any fat on it, then roast in a preheated oven at 230°C/450°F/ Gas Mark 8 for 10 minutes. Lower the heat to 180°C/350°F/Gas Mark 4 and continue roasting for 1 hour for medium, or 1¼ hours for well-done. Set the veal aside and leave to cool completely, reserving any juices in the roasting tin.

Meanwhile, drain the tuna, reserving the oil. Blend the eggs in a food processor with 1 teaspoon of the lemon juice and a pinch of salt. Add enough olive oil to the tuna oil to make up to 300 ml/10 fl oz.

With the motor running, add the oil to the eggs, drop by drop, until a thin mayonnaise forms. Add the tuna and process until smooth. Blend in lemon juice to taste. Adjust the seasoning.

Slice the cool meat very thinly. Add any juices to the reserved pan juices. Gradually pour the veal juices into the tuna mayonnaise, whisking until a thin, pouring consistency.

Layer the veal slices with the sauce on a platter, ending with a layer of sauce. Cover and leave to chill overnight. Garnish with olives, capers and a light sprinkling of parsley. Arrange lemon wedges around the edge and serve.

ROAST LAMB WITH GARLIC
AND ROSEMARY

1 LEG OF LAMB,
WEIGHING 1.5 KG/3 LB 5 OZ
6 GARLIC CLOVES, THINLY SLICED
LENGTHWAYS
8 FRESH ROSEMARY SPRIGS
SALT AND PEPPER
4 TBSP OLIVE OIL

GLAZE

4 TBSP REDCURRANT JELLY
300 ML/10 FL OZ ROSÉ WINE

SERVES 6

Preheat the oven to 200°C/400°F/Gas Mark 6. Using a small knife, cut slits all over the leg of lamb. Insert 1–2 garlic slices and 4–5 rosemary needles in each slit. Place any remaining rosemary in the base of a roasting tin. Season the lamb to taste with salt and pepper and place in the roasting tin. Pour over the oil. Cover with foil and roast for 1 hour 20 minutes.

Mix the redcurrant jelly and wine together in a small saucepan. Heat gently, stirring constantly, until combined. Bring to the boil, then reduce the heat and simmer until reduced. Remove the lamb from the oven and pour over the glaze. Return to the oven and cook uncovered for about 10 minutes, depending on how well done you like it.

Remove the lamb from the roasting tin, tent with foil and leave to rest for 15 minutes before carving and serving.

BAKED HAM WITH SAUCE

2–3 KG/4 LB 8 OZ–6 LB 8 OZ
LEAN GAMMON

2 BAY LEAVES

1–2 ONIONS, QUARTERED

2 CARROTS, THICKLY SLICED

6 CLOVES

GLAZE

1 TBSP REDCURRANT JELLY

1 TBSP WHOLEGRAIN MUSTARD

CUMBERLAND SAUCE

1 ORANGE

3 TBSP REDCURRANT JELLY

2 TBSP LEMON OR LIME JUICE

2 TBSP ORANGE JUICE

2–4 TBSP PORT

1 TBSP WHOLEGRAIN MUSTARD

TO GARNISH

SALAD LEAVES AND
ORANGE SLICES

SERVES 4-6

Place the meat in a large saucepan. Add the bay leaves, onions, carrots and cloves and cover with cold water. Bring to the boil over a low heat, cover and simmer for half the cooking time. To calculate the cooking time, allow 30 minutes per 500 g/1 lb 2 oz plus 30 minutes.

Preheat the oven to 180°C/350°F/Gas Mark 4. Drain the meat and remove the skin. Place the meat in a roasting tin and score the fat. To make the glaze, combine the ingredients and spread over the fat. Cook in the oven for the remainder of the cooking time. Baste at least once.

To make the sauce, pare the rind from half the orange and cut into strips. Cook in boiling water for 3 minutes. Drain.

Place all the remaining sauce ingredients in a small saucepan and heat gently, stirring occasionally, or until the redcurrant jelly dissolves. Add the orange rind strips and simmer gently for a further 3–4 minutes.

Slice the gammon and place on a warmed serving platter. Garnish with salad leaves and orange slices and serve with the Cumberland Sauce.

LAMB SHANKS BRAISED WITH GARLIC

1 TSP CORIANDER SEEDS

1 TSP CUMIN SEEDS

1 TSP GROUND CINNAMON

1 FRESH GREEN CHILLI,
DESEEDED AND FINELY CHOPPED

1 GARLIC BULB, SEPARATED INTO
CLOVES AND PEELED

125 ML/4 FL OZ GROUNDNUT OR
SUNFLOWER OIL

GRATED RIND OF 1 LIME

4 LAMB SHANKS

2 ONIONS, CHOPPED

2 CARROTS, CHOPPED

2 CELERY STICKS, CHOPPED

½ SMALL LIME, CHOPPED

ABOUT 700 ML/1¼ PINTS BEEF
STOCK OR WATER

1 TSP SUN-DRIED TOMATO PASTE

2 FRESH ROSEMARY SPRIGS

SALT AND PEPPER

TO GARNISH

2 FRESH MINT SPRIGS

SERVES 4

Dry-fry the seeds in a frying pan until fragrant. Combine the seeds, cinnamon, chilli and 2 garlic cloves in a mortar and pound with a pestle. Stir in half the oil and the lime rind. Rub over the lamb, cover and marinate in the refrigerator for 4 hours.

Preheat the oven to 200°C/400°F/Gas Mark 6. Heat the remaining oil in a frying pan. Brown the lamb all over and transfer to a flameproof casserole. Chop the remaining garlic. Add to the casserole dish with the onions, carrots, celery, lime and stock or water to cover. Stir in the tomato paste, herbs and season to taste with salt and pepper.

Cover and cook in the oven for 30 minutes. Reduce the temperature to 160°C/325°F/Gas Mark 3. Cook for a further 3 hours, or until very tender.

Transfer the lamb to a dish and keep warm. Strain the cooking juices into a saucepan. Boil until reduced. Pour over the lamb, garnish with mint and serve.

POT ROASTED LEG
OF LAMB

1.75 KG/3½ LB LEG OF LAMB

3–4 SPRIGS FRESH ROSEMARY

125 G/4½ OZ STREAKY
BACON RASHERS

4 TBSP OLIVE OIL

2–3 GARLIC CLOVES, CRUSHED

2 ONIONS, SLICED

2 CARROTS, SLICED

2 CELERY STALKS, SLICED

300 ML/½ PINT DRY WHITE WINE

1 TBSP TOMATO PURÉE

300 ML/½ PINT STOCK

350 G/12 OZ TOMATOES, PEELED,
QUARTERED AND DESEEDED

1 TBSP CHOPPED FRESH PARSLEY

1 TBSP CHOPPED FRESH OREGANO
OR MARJORAM

SALT AND PEPPER

TO GARNISH

FRESH ROSEMARY SPRIGS

SERVES 4

Wipe the joint of lamb all over, trimming off any excess fat, then season well with salt and pepper, rubbing well in. Lay the sprigs of rosemary over the lamb, cover evenly with the bacon rashers and tie in place with string.

Heat the oil in a frying pan and fry the lamb for about 10 minutes or until browned all over, turning several times. Remove from the pan.

Transfer the oil from the frying pan to a large fireproof casserole dish and fry the garlic and onion together for 3–4 minutes until beginning to soften. Add the carrots and celery and continue to cook for a few minutes longer.

Lay the lamb on top of the vegetables and press down to partly submerge. Pour the wine over the lamb, add the tomato purée and simmer for 3–4 minutes. Add the stock, tomatoes and herbs and seasoning and bring back to the boil for a further 3–4 minutes.

Cover the casserole dish tightly and cook in a moderate oven, 180°C/350°F/Gas Mark 4, for 2–2½ hours until very tender.

Remove the lamb from the casserole dish and if preferred, take off the bacon and herbs along with the string. Keep warm. Strain the juices, skimming off any excess fat, and serve in a jug. The vegetables may be put around the joint or in a serving dish. Garnish with fresh sprigs of rosemary.

RED ROAST PORK IN SOY SAUCE

450 G/1 LB LEAN PORK FILLETS

6 TBSP DARK SOY SAUCE

2 TBSP DRY SHERRY

1 TSP FIVE-SPICE POWDER

2 GARLIC CLOVES, CRUSHED

2.5 CM/1 INCH PIECE ROOT GINGER,
FINELY CHOPPED

1 LARGE RED PEPPER

1 LARGE YELLOW PEPPER

1 LARGE ORANGE PEPPER

4 TBSP CASTER SUGAR

2 TBSP RED WINE VINEGAR

TO GARNISH

SPRING ONIONS, SHREDDED AND
FRESH CHIVES, SNIPPED

SERVES 4

Trim away any excess fat and silver skin from the pork and place in a shallow dish.

Mix together the soy sauce, sherry, five-spice powder, garlic and ginger. Spoon over the pork, cover and marinate in the refrigerator for at least 1 hour or until required.

Preheat the oven to 190°C/375°F/Gas Mark 5. Drain the pork, reserving the marinade.

Place the pork on a roasting rack over a roasting tin. Cook in the oven, occasionally basting with the marinade, for 1 hour or until cooked through.

Meanwhile, halve and deseed the peppers. Cut each pepper half into 3 equal portions. Arrange them on a baking sheet and bake alongside the pork for the last 30 minutes of cooking time.

Place the caster sugar and vinegar in a saucepan and heat gently until the sugar dissolves. Bring to the boil and simmer for 3–4 minutes, until syrupy.

When the pork is cooked, remove it from the oven and brush with the sugar syrup. Leave for about 5 minutes, then slice and arrange on a serving platter with the peppers, garnished with the spring onions and chives.

Serve garnished with the spring onions and freshly snipped chives.

CYPRIOT LAMB WITH ORZO

2 LARGE GARLIC CLOVES

1 UNBONED SHOULDER OF LAMB

2 X 400 G/14 OZ CANS
CHOPPED TOMATOES

4 SPRIGS FRESH THYME

4 SPRIGS FRESH PARSLEY

1 BAY LEAF

120 ML/4 FL OZ WATER

250 G/9 OZ ORZO PASTA

SALT AND PEPPER

TO SERVE

FRESH THYME SPRIGS

SERVES 6

Cut the garlic cloves in half and remove the green cores, then thinly slice. Using the tip of a sharp knife, make slits all over the lamb shoulder, then insert the garlic slices into the slits.

Tip the tomatoes and their juices into a roasting tin large enough to hold the lamb shoulder. Add the thyme, parsley and bay leaf. Place the lamb on top, skin-side up, and cover the dish tightly with a sheet of foil, shiny side down. Scrunch the foil all around the edge so that none of the juices escape during cooking.

Put in a preheated oven at 160°C/325°F/Gas Mark 3 and cook for 3½–4 hours until the lamb is tender and the tomatoes are reduced to a thick sauce.

Remove the lamb from the roasting tin and set aside. Using a large metal spoon, skim off as much fat from the surface of the tomato sauce as possible.

Add the water and orzo to the tomatoes, stirring so the grains are submerged. Add a little extra water if the sauce seems too thick. Season to taste with salt and pepper. Return the lamb to the roasting tin.

Re-cover the roasting tin and return to the oven for 15 minutes, or until the orzo is tender. Remove the bay leaf. Leave the lamb to rest for 10 minutes, then slice and serve with the orzo in tomato juice, garnished with fresh thyme sprigs.

ROASTED RED
PORK

600 G/1 LB 5 OZ PORK FILLET

SERVES 4

MARINADE

2 GARLIC CLOVES, CRUSHED

1 TBSP FRESH ROOT GINGER, GRATED

1 TBSP LIGHT SOY SAUCE

1 TBSP THAI FISH SAUCE

1 TBSP RICE WINE

1 TBSP HOISIN SAUCE

1 TBSP SESAME OIL

1 TBSP PALM SUGAR OR SOFT BROWN SUGAR

½ TSP CHINESE FIVE-SPICE POWDER

A FEW DROPS RED FOOD COLOURING

TO GARNISH

RED CHILLI FLOWER

TO SERVE

CHINESE LEAVES, SHREDDED

Mix all the ingredients for the marinade together and spread the mixture over the pork, turning to coat evenly. Place in a large dish, cover and set aside in the refrigerator to marinate overnight.

Place a rack in a roasting tin, then half-fill the tin with boiling water. Lift the pork from the marinade and place on the rack. Reserve the marinade for later.

Roast in a preheated oven, 220°C/425°F/Gas Mark 7, for about 20 minutes. Baste with the reserved marinade, then lower the heat to 180°C/350°F/Gas Mark 4 and continue roasting for a further 35–40 minutes, basting occasionally with the marinade, until the pork is a rich reddish brown and thoroughly cooked.

Transfer the pork to a chopping board and cut into even slices. Arrange the slices on a bed of shredded Chinese leaves on a serving platter, garnish with a red chilli flower and serve immediately.

SAUERBRATEN

750 G/1 LB 10 OZ TOPSIDE OF BEEF,
TRIMMED OF ALL VISIBLE FAT

8 WHOLE CLOVES

1 TBSP SUNFLOWER OR CORN OIL

225 ML/8 FL OZ BEEF STOCK

1 KG/2 LB 4 OZ MIXED ROOT
VEGETABLES, SUCH AS CARROTS,
POTATOES AND SWEDE, PEELED
AND CUT INTO LARGE CHUNKS

2 TBSP RAISINS

1½ TSP CORNFLOUR

3 TBSP WATER

SALT AND PEPPER

MARINADE

200 ML/7 FL OZ WINE

5 TBSP RED WINE VINEGAR

1 ONION, CHOPPED

1½ TSP BROWN SUGAR

4 PEPPERCORNS

1 BAY LEAF

½ TSP GROUND MIXED SPICE

½ TSP MUSTARD

SERVES 4

To make the marinade, place all the ingredients, except the mustard, in a saucepan. Bring to simmering point, then remove from the heat and stir in the mustard. Stud the beef with cloves and place in a non-metallic dish. Pour the marinade over, cover and leave to cool, then chill in the refrigerator for 2 days. About 1 hour before cooking, remove the beef, pat dry and stand at room temperature. Reserve the marinade.

Preheat the oven to 150°C/300°F/Gas Mark 2. Heat the oil in a flameproof casserole dish, add the beef and cook over a medium heat for 5–10 minutes, or until browned. Pour the marinade into the casserole dish through a sieve, add the stock and bring to the boil. Cover and bake in the oven for 1 hour, turning and basting frequently with the cooking juices.

Meanwhile, blanch the vegetables in boiling water for 3 minutes, then drain. Arrange the vegetables around the beef, return to the oven and cook for 1 hour, or until the beef is very tender and the vegetables are cooked.

Transfer the beef and vegetables to a serving dish. Place the casserole dish on a low heat and add the raisins. Mix the cornflour and water until smooth and stir into the cooking juices. Bring to the boil, stirring, then simmer for 2–3 minutes. Season and serve.

ROAST GAMMON

1.3 KG/3 LB BONELESS GAMMON,
PRE-SOAKED IF NECESSARY
2 TBSP DIJON MUSTARD
85 G/3 OZ DEMERARA SUGAR
½ TSP GROUND CINNAMON
½ TSP GROUND GINGER
18 WHOLE CLOVES

SERVES 6

Place the joint in a large saucepan, cover with cold water and slowly bring to the boil over a gentle heat. Cover and simmer very gently for 1 hour.

Preheat the oven to 200°C/400°F/Gas Mark 6.

CUMBERLAND SAUCE

USING A LEMON ZESTER, REMOVE THE ZEST OF 2 ORANGES. PLACE 4 TABLESPOONS REDCURRANT JELLY IN A SMALL SAUCEPAN WITH 4 TABLESPOONS PORT AND 1 TEASPOON MUSTARD AND HEAT GENTLY UNTIL THE JELLY IS MELTED. CUT THE ORANGES IN HALF AND SQUEEZE THE JUICE INTO THE PAN. ADD THE ORANGE ZEST AND SEASON WITH SALT AND PEPPER TO TASTE. SERVE COLD WITH GAMMON. THE SAUCE CAN BE KEPT IN A SCREW-TOP JAR IN THE REFRIGERATOR FOR UP TO 2 WEEKS.

Remove the gammon from the pan and drain. Remove the rind from the gammon and discard. Score the fat into a diamond-shaped pattern with a sharp knife.

Spread the mustard over the fat. Mix together the sugar and the spices on a plate and roll the gammon in it, pressing down well to coat evenly.

Stud the diamond shapes with cloves and place the joint in a roasting tin. Roast for 20 minutes until the glaze is a rich golden colour.

To serve hot, allow to stand for 20 minutes before carving. If the gammon is to be served cold, it can be cooked a day ahead. Serve with Cumberland sauce.

ROAST LAMB WITH ROSEMARY AND MARSALA

1.8 KG/4 LB LEG OF LAMB

2 GARLIC CLOVES, SLICED THINLY

2 TBSP ROSEMARY LEAVES

8 TBSP OLIVE OIL

SALT AND PEPPER

900 G/2 LB POTATOES,
CUT INTO 2.5 CM/1 INCH CUBES

6 FRESH SAGE LEAVES, CHOPPED

150 ML/¼ PINT MARSALA

SERVES 6

Use a small, sharp knife to make incisions all over the lamb, opening them out slightly to make little pockets. Insert the garlic slices and about half the rosemary leaves in the pockets.

Place the lamb in a roasting tin and spoon half the olive oil over it. Roast in a preheated oven, 220°C/425°F/Gas Mark 7, for 15 minutes.

Lower the oven temperature to 180°C/350°/Gas Mark 4. Remove the lamb from the oven and season to taste with salt and pepper. Turn the lamb over, return to the oven and roast for a further hour.

Meanwhile, spread out the cubed potatoes in a second roasting tin, pour the remaining olive oil over them and toss to coat. Sprinkle with the remaining rosemary and the sage. Place the potatoes in the oven with the lamb and roast for 40 minutes.

Remove the lamb from the oven, turn it over and pour over the Marsala. Return it to the oven with the potatoes and cook for a further 15 minutes.

Transfer the lamb to a carving board and cover with foil. Place the roasting tin over a high heat and bring the juices to the boil. Continue to boil until thickened and syrupy. Strain into a warmed sauce boat or jug.

Carve the lamb into slices and serve with the potatoes and sauce.

STUFFED ROAST PORK
WITH GARLIC

1 KG/2 LB 4 OZ PORK LOIN,
BACKBONE REMOVED AND
RIND SCORED
2 TBSP HONEY

STUFFING
85 G/3 OZ BUTTER
1 GARLIC CLOVE, CHOPPED
2 SHALLOTS, CHOPPED
75 G/2¾ OZ MUSHROOMS, CHOPPED
4 RASHERS LEAN BACK BACON,
CHOPPED
100 G/3½ OZ FRESH BREADCRUMBS
1 TBSP FINELY CHOPPED
FRESH SAGE
1 TBSP LEMON JUICE
1 TBSP GRATED LEMON RIND
SALT AND PEPPER

TO GARNISH
SPRIGS OF FRESH SAGE

TO SERVE
ROAST POTATOES

SERVES 4

Preheat the oven to 230°C/450°F/Gas Mark 8. To make the stuffing, melt the butter in a saucepan over a medium heat. Add the garlic and shallots and cook, stirring, for 3 minutes, or until softened. Add the mushrooms and bacon, and cook for another 2 minutes. Remove from the heat and stir in the breadcrumbs, sage, lemon juice and rind, and salt and pepper to taste.

Put the stuffing in the middle of the pork loin, then roll up and secure the loin with several lengths of tied string. Place the joint in a roasting tin, then rub the skin with plenty of salt and season with pepper. Brush the honey over the pork.

Cook in the preheated oven for 25 minutes, then reduce the heat to 180°C/350°F/Gas Mark 4. Cook, basting occasionally, for about 1¼ hours, or until cooked through. Remove from the oven and leave to rest for 15 minutes. Garnish with sage sprigs and serve with roast potatoes.

FESTIVE BEEF
WELLINGTON

750 G/1 LB 10 OZ THICK BEEF FILLET

2 TBSP BUTTER

SALT AND PEPPER

2 TBSP VEGETABLE OIL

1 GARLIC CLOVE, CHOPPED

1 ONION, CHOPPED

175 G/6 OZ CHESTNUT MUSHROOMS

1 TBSP CHOPPED FRESH SAGE

SALT AND PEPPER

350 G/12 OZ FROZEN PUFF PASTRY, DEFROSTED

1 EGG, BEATEN

TO GARNISH

CHOPPED FRESH SAGE

SERVES 4

Preheat the oven to 220°C/425°F/Gas Mark 7. Put the beef in a roasting tin, spread with butter and season. Roast for 30 minutes, then remove from the oven. Meanwhile, heat the oil in a pan over a medium heat. Add the garlic and onion and cook, stirring, for 3 minutes. Stir in the mushrooms, sage and seasoning and cook for 5 minutes. Remove from the heat.

Roll out the pastry into a rectangle large enough to enclose the beef, then place the beef in the middle and spread the mushroom mixture over it. Bring the long sides of the pastry together over the beef and seal with beaten egg. Tuck the short ends over (trim away excess pastry) and seal. Place on a baking sheet, seam-side down. Make 2 slits in the top. Decorate with dough shapes and brush with beaten egg. Bake for 40 minutes. If the pastry browns too quickly, cover with foil. Remove from the oven, garnish with sage.

MAPLE ROAST LAMB
WITH CIDER

2 TBSP LEMON-FLAVOURED OIL OR
EXTRA-VIRGIN OLIVE OIL

2.25 KG/5 LB LEG OF LAMB

1 GARLIC CLOVE, CHOPPED

1 TBSP CHOPPED FRESH OREGANO

JUICE OF 1 LEMON

3 TBSP MAPLE SYRUP

SALT AND PEPPER

700 ML/1¼ PINTS DRY CIDER

1 TBSP CORNFLOUR

2 TBSP WATER

TO GARNISH

SPRIGS OF FRESH OREGANO

TO SERVE

ROAST POTATOES

SERVES 4

Preheat the oven to 200°C/400°F/Gas Mark 6. Pour the oil into a roasting tin. Using a sharp knife, trim off and discard any excess fat from the lamb, then make small incisions all over. Transfer the joint to the roasting tin. Put the garlic into a bowl and add the chopped oregano, lemon juice, maple syrup, and salt and pepper to taste. Mix together well. Pour the mixture evenly over the lamb, pushing it into the incisions, then pour over the cider.

Transfer the tin to the preheated oven and roast for 30 minutes, turning once and basting occasionally. Reduce the oven temperature to 150°C/300°F/Gas Mark 2 and cook for a further 2¾ hours, or until tender and cooked through. Lift out and place on a serving platter to rest for 10 minutes. Blend the cornflour with the water, then stir into the juices in the tin. Transfer to the stove. Stir over a low heat until thickened. Garnish the lamb with oregano sprigs. Serve with roast potatoes and the thickened juices.

LAMB SHANKS WITH ROASTED ONIONS

4 X 350 G/12 OZ LAMB SHANKS

6 GARLIC CLOVES

2 TBSP VIRGIN OLIVE OIL

1 TBSP VERY FINELY CHOPPED
FRESH ROSEMARY

PEPPER

4 RED ONIONS

SALT

350 G/12 OZ CARROTS,
CUT INTO THIN BATONS

4 TBSP WATER

SERVES 4

Trim off any excess fat from the lamb. Using a small, sharp knife, make 6 incisions in each shank. Cut the garlic cloves lengthways into 4 slices. Insert 6 garlic slices in the incisions in each lamb shank.

Place the lamb in a single layer in a roasting tin, drizzle with the olive oil, sprinkle with the rosemary and season with pepper. Roast in a preheated oven, 180°C/350°F/Gas Mark 4, for 45 minutes.

Wrap each of the onions in a square of foil. Remove the roasting tin from the oven and season the lamb shanks with salt. Return the tin to the oven and place the wrapped onions on the shelf next to it. Roast for a further 1-1¼ hours, until the lamb is very tender.

Meanwhile, bring a large saucepan of water to the boil. Add the carrot batons and blanch for 1 minute. Drain and refresh under cold water.

Remove the roasting tin from the oven when the lamb is meltingly tender and transfer it to a warmed serving dish. Skim off any fat from the roasting tin and place it over a medium heat. Add the carrots and cook for 2 minutes, then add the water, bring to the boil and simmer, stirring constantly and scraping up the glazed bits from the base of the roasting tin.

Transfer the carrots and sauce to the serving dish. Remove the onions from the oven and unwrap. Cut off and discard about 1 cm/½ inch of the tops and add the onions to the dish. Serve immediately.

MARINATED ROAST LAMB

425 ML/15 FL OZ NATURAL YOGURT

125 ML/4 FL OZ LEMON JUICE

3 TBSP MALT VINEGAR

2 TSP CHILLI POWDER

2 TSP GINGER PASTE

2 TSP GARLIC PASTE

1 TSP BROWN SUGAR

1 TSP SALT

FEW DROPS RED FOOD COLOURING

2.5 KG/5 LB 8 OZ LEG OF LAMB

VEGETABLE OIL, FOR BRUSHING

TO GARNISH

FRESH CORIANDER SPRIGS

SERVES 6

Mix the yogurt, lemon juice, vinegar, chilli powder, ginger paste, garlic paste, sugar, salt and food colouring together in a bowl. Make several deep gashes all over the lamb and place in a large, roasting tin. Pour over the yogurt mixture, turning to coat and pressing it well into the gashes. Cover with clingfilm and leave to marinate in the refrigerator for 8 hours or overnight.

Preheat the oven to 190°C/375°F/Gas Mark 5. Remove the lamb from the refrigerator and bring to room temperature. Roast the lamb in the preheated oven for 1¼ hours, basting occasionally with the marinade.

Remove the lamb from the oven and reduce the oven temperature to 160°C/325°F/Gas Mark 3. Place the lamb on a large sheet of foil, brush with vegetable oil, then wrap the foil around the meat to enclose it completely. Return to the oven and roast for a further 45–60 minutes, or until tender.

Leave the lamb to rest for 10 minutes before carving and serving, garnished with fresh coriander sprigs.

ROAST LAMB WITH BEANS

225 G/8 OZ DRIED
FLAGEOLET BEANS

1 LARGE ONION, QUARTERED

6 LARGE GARLIC CLOVES

1 BAY LEAF

SPRIGS OF FRESH ROSEMARY

900 G/2 LB BONELESS LEG OF
LAMB, ROLLED AND TIED

2 TSP OLIVE OIL

40 G/1½ OZ UNSALTED BUTTER

2 TBSP CHOPPED FRESH
FLAT-LEAF PARSLEY

150 ML/5 FL OZ MEDIUM-DRY CIDER

ABOUT 150 ML/5 FL OZ LAMB
STOCK OR VEGETABLE STOCK

SALT AND PEPPER

SERVES 4-6

Put the beans in a large bowl, add enough water to cover by 2.5 cm/1 inch and leave to soak overnight.

The next day, drain and rinse the beans. Place the beans in a large saucepan and cover with twice their depth of water. Turn the heat to high, bring the water to the boil, skimming the surface as necessary, and boil for 10 minutes.

Drain the beans, then re-cover with more water and return to the boil. Add the onion, 4 of the garlic cloves and the bay leaf. Reduce the heat to low, cover the saucepan and leave to simmer for 60–90 minutes, or until the beans are tender. The exact cooking time will depend on how old the beans are; older beans will take longer to cook.

Meanwhile, heat the oven to 180°C/350°F/Gas Mark 4. Cut the remaining 2 cloves of garlic into thin slivers. Insert a couple of rosemary sprigs into the centre of the rolled lamb. Use the tip of a knife to make thin cuts all over the lamb, then insert the garlic slivers. Rub the lamb all over with the oil and season to taste with salt and pepper. Scatter over some rosemary leaves.

Place the lamb on a rack in a roasting tin and roast for 1 hour.

When the beans are tender, drain them well and discard the onion, garlic and bay leaf. Stir in the butter, parsley and salt and pepper to taste. Cover the beans with foil, shiny-side down, and keep warm.

When the lamb is cooked, transfer it to a serving platter, cover with foil and set aside to rest for 10 minutes. Meanwhile, remove the rack, tilt the roasting tin and use a large metal spoon to remove the fat from the surface of the pan juices.

Place the tin over a medium-high heat and deglaze it by stirring in the cider and scraping the sediment from the base of the pan. Bring to the boil and continue boiling until the juices reduce slightly, then add the stock and continue boiling until reduced by half. Season to taste with salt and pepper. Thinly slice the lamb and serve with the beans and pan juices.

ROAST BEEF

2.7 KG/6 LB PRIME RIB OF BEEF

SALT AND PEPPER

2 TSP DRY ENGLISH MUSTARD

3 TBSP PLAIN FLOUR

300 ML/½ PINT RED WINE

300 ML/½ PINT BEEF STOCK

2 TSP WORCESTERSHIRE SAUCE

YORKSHIRE PUDDING

SERVES 4

PREHEAT THE OVEN TO
220°C/425°F/GAS MARK 7.
MAKE A BATTER WITH 100 G/3½ OZ
PLAIN FLOUR, A PINCH OF SALT,
1 BEATEN EGG AND 300 ML/10 FL OZ
MILK AND WATER MIXED. ALLOW
TO STAND FOR HALF AN HOUR.
HEAT 2 TBSP ROAST BEEF DRIPPING
OR OLIVE OIL IN A 20-CM/8-INCH
SQUARE ROASTING TIN IN THE TOP
OF THE OVEN. REMOVE THE TIN
FROM THE OVEN, POUR IN THE
BATTER AND BAKE FOR
25-30 MINUTES UNTIL IT IS
PUFFED UP AND GOLDEN BROWN.

TO SERVE

YORKSHIRE PUDDING

SERVES 8

Preheat the oven to 230°C/450°F/Gas Mark 8.

Season the meat with the salt and pepper and rub in the mustard and 1 tablespoon of the flour.

Place the meat in a roasting tin large enough to hold it comfortably and roast for 15 minutes. Reduce the heat to 190°C/375°F/Gas Mark 5 and cook for 15 minutes per 450 g/1 lb, plus 15 minutes (1 hour 45 minutes for this joint) for rare beef or 20 minutes per 450 g/1 lb, plus 20 minutes (2 hours 20 minutes) for medium beef. Baste the meat from time to time to keep it moist and if the tin becomes too dry, add a little stock or red wine.

Remove the meat from the oven and place on a hot serving plate, cover with foil and leave in a warm place for 10–15 minutes.

To make the gravy, pour off most of the fat from the tin (reserve it for the Yorkshire pudding), leaving behind the meat juices and the sediment. Place the tin on the top of the stove over a medium heat and scrape all the sediments from the base of the tin. Sprinkle in the remaining flour and quickly mix it into the juices with a small whisk. When you have a smooth paste, gradually add the wine and most of the stock, whisking all the time. Bring to the boil, then turn down the heat to a gentle simmer and cook for 2–3 minutes. Season with salt and pepper and add the remaining stock, if needed, and a little Worcestershire sauce.

When ready to serve, carve the meat into slices and serve on hot plates. Pour the gravy into a warm jug and take direct to the table. Serve with Yorkshire pudding.

POT-ROAST
PORK

1 TBSP SUNFLOWER OIL

55 G/2 OZ BUTTER

1 KG/2 LB 4 OZ BONED AND
ROLLED PORK LOIN JOINT

4 SHALLOTS, CHOPPED

6 JUNIPER BERRIES

2 FRESH THYME SPRIGS,
PLUS EXTRA TO GARNISH

150 ML/5 FL OZ DRY CIDER

150 ML/5 FL OZ CHICKEN STOCK OR
WATER

SALT AND PEPPER

8 CELERY STICKS, CHOPPED

2 TBSP PLAIN FLOUR

150 ML/5 FL OZ DOUBLE CREAM

TO SERVE

FRESHLY COOKED PEAS

SERVES 4

Heat the oil with half the butter in a heavy-based saucepan or flameproof casserole dish. Add the pork and cook over a medium heat, turning frequently, for 5–10 minutes, or until browned. Transfer to a plate.

Add the shallots to the saucepan and cook, stirring frequently, for 5 minutes, or until softened. Add the juniper berries and thyme sprigs and return the pork to the saucepan, with any juices that have collected on the plate. Pour in the cider and stock, season to taste with salt and pepper, then cover and simmer for 30 minutes. Turn the pork over and add the celery. Re-cover the pan and cook for a further 40 minutes.

Meanwhile, make a beurre manié by mashing the remaining butter with the flour in a small bowl. Transfer the pork and celery to a platter with a slotted spoon and keep warm. Remove and discard the juniper berries and thyme. Whisk the beurre manié, a little at a time, into the simmering cooking liquid. Cook, stirring constantly, for 2 minutes, then stir in the cream and bring to the boil. Slice the pork and spoon a little of the sauce over it. Garnish with thyme sprigs and serve immediately with the celery and freshly cooked peas. Serve the remaining sauce separately.

4 RIBS

Ribs smothered in a sticky sauce, whether cooked on the
barbecue, in the oven or under the grill, are always fun, not least
because you can eat them with your fingers and have the
perfect excuse for behaving like a child. They also taste great, whether
Hot & Spicy Ribs (see page 176), Chinese Ribs (see page 184) or Spare
Ribs with Chilli (see page 196). This chapter also includes recipes for
those with more adult and sophisticated tastes, such as Crusted Rack of
Lamb (see page 178) and Lamb with Balsamic & Rosemary Marinade
(see page 200).

HOT AND SPICY RIBS

1 ONION, CHOPPED

2 GARLIC CLOVES, CHOPPED

2.5-CM/1-INCH PIECE FRESH ROOT
GINGER, SLICED

1 FRESH RED CHILLI, DESEEDED
AND CHOPPED

5 TBSP DARK SOY SAUCE

3 TBSP LIME JUICE

1 TBSP PALM OR
MUSCOVADO SUGAR

2 TBSP GROUNDNUT OIL

SALT AND PEPPER

1 KG/2 LB 4 OZ PORK SPARE RIBS,
SEPARATED

SERVES 4

Preheat the barbecue. Put the onion, garlic, ginger, chilli and soy sauce into a food processor and process to a paste. Transfer to a jug and stir in the lime juice, sugar and oil and season to taste with salt and pepper.

Place the spare ribs in a preheated wok or large, heavy-based saucepan and pour in the soy sauce mixture. Place on the hob and bring to the boil, then simmer over a low heat, stirring frequently, for 30 minutes. If the mixture appears to be drying out, add a little water.

Remove the spare ribs, reserving the sauce. Cook the ribs over medium hot coals, turning and basting frequently with the sauce, for 20–30 minutes. Transfer to a large serving plate and serve immediately.

Alternative Cooking Method
A griddle pan or frying pan can also be used to cook these ribs. Ensure that you brush the pan with a little oil first and then pre-heat before adding the meat. Cooking times may be increased slightly as this method of cooking does not generate the high heat of a barbecue. You therefore will need to look for visual signs that the food is cooked to your liking.

CRUSTED RACK OF LAMB

2 RACKS OF LAMB,
ABOUT 6–8 CHOPS EACH, SKIN
REMOVED, TRIMMED OF ANY
EXCESS FAT
40 G/1½ OZ FRESH WHOLEMEAL
BREADCRUMBS
2–3 GARLIC CLOVES, CRUSHED
2 TBSP CHOPPED FRESH PARSLEY
1 TBSP CHOPPED FRESH MINT
1 TBSP FINELY GRATED
LEMON RIND
SALT AND PEPPER
1 EGG

FOR THE SALSA

1 SMALL GREEN DESSERT APPLE,
WASHED, CORED AND FINELY DICED
2 TOMATOES, DESEEDED AND
FINELY DICED
3 SPRING ONIONS, FINELY CHOPPED
1 TBSP CHOPPED FRESH MINT

FOR THE MASH

450 G/1 LB SWEET POTATOES,
PEELED AND CHOPPED
2 TBSP MILK
1 TBSP CHOPPED FRESH MINT

TO SERVE

LIGHTLY COOKED GREEN VEGETABLE,
SUCH AS BROCCOLI

SERVES 4

Preheat the oven to 190°C/375°F/Gas Mark 5. Wipe the lamb racks with kitchen paper and wrap the ends of the bones with foil.

Mix the breadcrumbs, garlic, herbs, lemon rind and salt and pepper to taste together in a bowl and bind with the egg. Press on to the skinned side of the lamb. Stand the racks in a roasting tin and roast in the preheated oven for 40–50 minutes, or until cooked to your personal preference.

Remove from the oven, remove and discard the foil from the bones and cover with a sheet of foil. Leave to rest for 5 minutes.

Meanwhile, mix all the salsa ingredients together in a small serving bowl, cover and reserve until required.

Cook the sweet potatoes in a saucepan of lightly salted boiling water for 15–20 minutes, or until tender when pierced with a fork. Drain, mash, then beat in the milk and mint until smooth. Serve the lamb racks with the salsa and mash, accompanied by a lightly cooked green vegetable, such as broccoli.

RACK OF LAMB

1 TRIMMED RACK OF LAMB
(APPROXIMATELY
250–300 G/9–10 OZ RACK)
1 GARLIC CLOVE, CRUSHED
150 ML/¼ PINT RED WINE
1 SPRIG OF FRESH ROSEMARY,
CRUSHED
SALT AND PEPPER
1 TBSP OLIVE OIL
150 ML/¼ PINT LAMB STOCK
2 TBSP REDCURRANT JELLY

MINT SAUCE

CHOP A SMALL BUNCH OF FRESH
MINT LEAVES WITH 2 TEASPOONS
CASTER SUGAR AND PLACE IN A
SMALL BOWL. ADD 2 TABLESPOONS
BOILING WATER AND STIR TO
DISSOLVE THE SUGAR. ADD
2 TABLESPOONS WHITE WINE
VINEGAR AND LEAVE TO STAND
FOR 30 MINUTES BEFORE SERVING
WITH THE LAMB.

SERVES 2

Place the rack of lamb in a non-metallic bowl and rub all over with the garlic. Pour over the wine and place the rosemary sprig on top. Cover and leave to marinate in the fridge for 3 hours or overnight if possible.

Preheat the oven to 220°C/425°F/Gas Mark 7.

Remove the lamb from the marinade, reserving the marinade, dry the meat with kitchen paper and season well with salt and pepper. Put in a small roasting tin, drizzle with the oil and roast for 15–20 minutes, depending on whether you like your meat pink or medium. Remove the lamb from the oven and leave to rest, covered with foil, in a warm place for 5 minutes.

Put the marinade into a small pan, bring to the boil over a medium heat and bubble away for 2–3 minutes. Add the lamb stock and redcurrant jelly and simmer until a syrupy consistency is achieved.

Carve the lamb into cutlets and serve on warmed plates with the sauce spooned over the top. Serve the mint sauce separately.

BARBECUED LAMB RIBS

BREAST OF LAMB,
ABOUT 700 G/1 LB 9 OZ
3 TBSP SWEET CHUTNEY
4 TBSP TOMATO KETCHUP
2 TBSP CIDER VINEGAR
2 TSP WORCESTERSHIRE SAUCE
2 TSP MILD MUSTARD
1 TBSP LIGHT MUSCOVADO SUGAR

TO SERVE

SALAD LEAVES AND
CHERRY TOMATOES

SERVES 4

Preheat the barbecue. Using a sharp knife, cut between the ribs of the breast of lamb to divide it into slightly smaller pieces.

Bring a large saucepan of water to the boil. Add the lamb and parboil for 5 minutes. Remove the meat from the water and pat dry thoroughly with kitchen paper.

Mix the sweet chutney, tomato ketchup, cider vinegar, Worcestershire sauce, mustard and sugar together in a shallow, non-metallic dish to make a sauce.

Using a sharp knife, cut the lamb into individual ribs. Add the ribs to the sauce and toss until well coated. Remove the ribs from the sauce, reserving the remaining sauce for basting. Cook the ribs over hot coals for 10–15 minutes, turning and basting frequently with the reserved sauce.

Transfer the ribs to warmed serving plates. Serve immediately with salad leaves and cherry tomatoes.

CHINESE RIBS

1 KG/2 LB 4 OZ PORK SPARE RIBS, SEPARATED

4 TBSP DARK SOY SAUCE

3 TBSP MUSCOVADO SUGAR

1 TBSP GROUNDNUT OR SUNFLOWER OIL

2 GARLIC CLOVES, FINELY CHOPPED

2 TSP CHINESE FIVE-SPICE POWDER

1-CM/½-INCH PIECE FRESH ROOT GINGER, GRATED

TO GARNISH

SHREDDED SPRING ONIONS

SERVES 4

Place the spare ribs in a large, shallow, non-metallic dish. Mix the soy sauce, sugar, oil, garlic, Chinese five-spice powder and ginger together in a bowl. Pour the mixture over the ribs and turn until the ribs are thoroughly coated in the marinade.

Cover the dish with clingfilm and leave to marinate in the refrigerator for at least 6 hours.

Preheat the barbecue. Drain the ribs, reserving the marinade. Cook over medium hot coals, turning and brushing frequently with the reserved marinade, for 30–40 minutes. Transfer to a large serving dish, garnish with the shredded spring onions and serve immediately.

Alternative Cooking Method

A griddle pan or frying pan can also be used to cook these ribs. Ensure that you brush the pan with a little oil first and then pre-heat before adding the meat. Cooking times may be increased slightly as this method of cooking does not generate the high heat of a barbecue. You therefore will need to look for visual signs that the food is cooked to your liking.

TANGY PORK RIBS

1¼ TSP SALT

2 TSP PAPRIKA

2 TSP PEPPER

1.3 KG/3 LB PORK RIBS

1 TBSP CHILLI OR VEGETABLE OIL

1 ONION, FINELY CHOPPED

6 SPRING ONIONS, TRIMMED
AND CHOPPED

3 GARLIC CLOVES, CHOPPED

2 TSP FINELY CHOPPED FRESH
GINGER ROOT

1 RED CHILLI, CHOPPED

1 TBSP CHOPPED FRESH
CORIANDER

1 TBSP CHOPPED
FLAT-LEAF PARSLEY

1 TBSP SWEET SHERRY

1½ TBSP BROWN SUGAR

4 TBSP CHINESE
CHILLI BEAN SAUCE

1 TBSP TOMATO PURÉE

1 TBSP RICE WINE

1 TBSP SHERRY VINEGAR

100 ML/3½ FL OZ ORANGE JUICE

2½ TBSP SOY SAUCE

SALT AND PEPPER

TO SERVE

WEDGES OF ORANGE

SERVES 4

Preheat the oven to 240°C/475°F/Gas Mark 9. Combine the salt, paprika and pepper in a baking dish and then add the ribs. Turn them in the dish to coat them well all over. Cook in the centre of the preheated oven for 1¾–2 hours, then remove the dish from the oven, lift out the ribs, drain off the fat and set aside.

Heat the oil in a frying pan. Add the onion, spring onions, garlic, ginger and chilli and stir-fry over a high heat for 1 minute. Then add the herbs, sherry, sugar, chilli bean sauce, tomato purée, rice wine, vinegar, orange juice and soy sauce. Stir in a large pinch of salt and season well with pepper. Bring to the boil, lower the heat and simmer for 15–20 minutes, stirring occasionally.

Alternative Cooking Method

To barbecue the ribs, coat them in the sauce, then grill them over hot coals for 7–10 minutes on each side, or until cooked right through, turning them frequently and basting with more sauce as necessary. Serve at once, accompanied by orange wedges.

BARBECUED SPICY PORK RIBS

900 G/2 LB PORK SPARE RIBS

150 ML/5 FL OZ PASSATA

2 TBSP RED WINE VINEGAR

2 TBSP DARK MUSCOVADO SUGAR

1 GARLIC CLOVE, CRUSHED

1 TSP DRIED THYME

½ TSP DRIED ROSEMARY

1 TSP CHILLI SAUCE

TO GARNISH

FRESH RED CHILLIES

TO SERVE

MIXED SALAD LEAVES

SERVES 8

If you buy the spare ribs in a single piece, carefully cut them into individual ribs using a very sharp knife. Bring a large saucepan of water to the boil and add the ribs. Cook the ribs for 10 minutes, then drain them thoroughly. Place the ribs in a large, shallow, non-metallic dish.

To make the spicy sauce, mix the passata, red wine vinegar, sugar, garlic, dried thyme, dried rosemary and chilli sauce together in a bowl until well blended.

Pour the sauce over the pork ribs and toss to coat on all sides. Cover and leave to marinate in the refrigerator for 1 hour.

Preheat the barbecue. Remove the ribs from the sauce, reserving the sauce for basting. Cook the ribs over hot coals for 5–10 minutes, then move them to a cooler part of the barbecue. Cook for a further 15–20 minutes, turning and basting frequently with the remaining sauce. Transfer the ribs to warmed serving plates and garnish with the red chillies. Serve immediately with mixed salad leaves.

SPARE RIBS IN
BARBECUE SAUCE

500 G/1 LB 2 OZ PORK FINGER
SPARE RIBS

1 TBSP SUGAR

1 TBSP LIGHT SOY SAUCE

1 TBSP DARK SOY SAUCE

3 TBSP HOI-SIN SAUCE

1 TBSP RICE WINE OR DRY SHERRY

4-5 TBSP WATER OR
CHINESE STOCK

MILD CHILLI SAUCE, TO DIP

TO GARNISH

CORIANDER LEAVES

SERVES 4

Using a sharp knife, trim off any excess fat from the spare ribs and cut into pieces. Place the ribs in a baking dish.

Mix together the sugar, light and dark soy sauce, hoi-sin sauce and wine. Pour over the ribs in the baking dish. Turn to coat the ribs thoroughly in the mixture and leave to marinate for about 2-3 hours.

Add the water or Chinese stock to the ribs and spread them out in the dish. Roast in a preheated hot oven for 15 minutes.

Turn the ribs over, lower the oven temperature and cook for 30-35 minutes longer.

To serve, chop each rib into 3-4 small, bite-sized pieces with a large knife or Chinese cleaver and arrange neatly on a serving dish.

Pour the sauce from the baking dish over the spare ribs and garnish with a few coriander leaves. Place some mild chilli sauce into a small dish and serve with the ribs as a dip. Serve immediately.

SPICY RACK OF LAMB
WITH HUMMUS

6 RACKS OF LAMB,
EACH WITH 3 CUTLETS

2 TBSP OLIVE OIL

MARINADE

1 TBSP OLIVE OIL

2 TBSP CLEAR HONEY

2 TSP GROUND CORIANDER

2 TSP GROUND CUMIN

1 TSP GROUND ALLSPICE

½ TSP PAPRIKA

TO GARNISH

FEW SPRIGS OF FRESH MINT

TO SERVE

HUMMUS

SERVES 6

Preheat the oven to 190°C/375°F/Gas Mark 5. Put the lamb in a roasting tin and spoon over 2 tbsp of olive oil. Roast for 10–15 minutes, or until almost cooked through.

Mix together 1 tbsp of olive oil, the honey, coriander, cumin, allspice and paprika in a small bowl. Brush the spice mixture all over the warm lamb, then place in a dish and leave to cool. Cover with clingfilm and marinate in the refrigerator overnight.

Cook the lamb on a medium barbecue, turning frequently, until heated through and well browned. Alternatively place the lamb into a preheated oven to 220°C/425°F/Gas Mark 7 until heated through and well browned. Transfer to 6 serving plates, add 2–3 tbsp hummus to each, garnish with mint sprigs and serve.

SWEET AND SOUR RIBS

4 SPRING ONIONS,
FINELY CHOPPED

3 TBSP LEMON JUICE

150 ML/5 FL OZ WHITE
WINE VINEGAR

2 TSP ENGLISH MUSTARD

3 TBSP MUSCOVADO SUGAR

3 TBSP WORCESTERSHIRE SAUCE

5 TBSP SUN-DRIED TOMATO PASTE

1 KG/2 LB 4 OZ PORK SPARERIBS

SALT AND PEPPER

SERVES 4

Put the spring onions, lemon juice, vinegar, mustard, sugar, Worcestershire sauce and sun-dried tomato paste in a saucepan, season with salt and pepper and bring to the boil, stirring well to mix. Reduce the heat and simmer, stirring occasionally, for 30 minutes. Transfer the saucepan to the side of the barbecue.

Using a sharp knife, make deep scores all over the racks of ribs, then brush them all over with the sauce.

Grill over a medium barbecue, turning and brushing frequently with the sauce, for 1–1¼ hours, or until cooked through and tender. Serve immediately.

SPARE RIBS WITH CHILLI

500 G/1 LB 2 OZ PORK SPARE RIBS

1 TSP SUGAR

1 TBSP LIGHT SOY SAUCE

1 TSP RICE WINE OR DRY SHERRY

1 TSP CORNFLOUR

ABOUT 600 ML/1 PINT
VEGETABLE OIL

1 GARLIC CLOVE, FINELY CHOPPED

1 SPRING ONION,
CUT INTO SHORT SECTIONS

1 SMALL HOT CHILLI PEPPER
(GREEN OR RED), THINLY SLICED

2 TBSP BLACK BEAN SAUCE

ABOUT 150 ML/¼ PINT
CHINESE STOCK OR WATER

1 SMALL ONION, DICED

1 MEDIUM GREEN PEPPER, CORED,
SEEDED AND DICED

SERVES 4

Trim any excess fat from the ribs. Using a sharp knife or meat cleaver, chop each rib into 3-4 bite-sized piecess and place in a shallow dish.

Mix together the sugar, soy sauce, wine and cornflour and pour the mixture over the pork ribs. Leave to marinate for 35-45 minutes.

Heat the vegetable oil in a large preheated wok or frying pan.

Add the spare ribs to the wok and deep-fry for 2-3 minutes until light brown. Remove with a slotted spoon and drain on absorbent kitchen paper.

Pour off the oil, leaving about 1 tablespoon in the wok. Add the garlic, spring onion, chilli pepper and black bean sauce and stir-fry for 30-40 seconds.

Add the spare ribs, blend well, then add the stock or water. Bring to the boil, then reduce the heat, cover and braise for 8-10 minutes, stirring once or twice.

Add the onion and green pepper, increase the heat to high, and stir uncovered for about 2 minutes to reduce the sauce a little. Serve hot.

ROASTED SPARE RIBS WITH
HONEY AND SOY

1 KG/2 LB 4 OZ CHINESE-STYLE
SPARE RIBS

½ LEMON

½ SMALL ORANGE

2.5 CM/1 IN PIECE FRESH ROOT
GINGER, PEELED

2 GARLIC CLOVES, PEELED

1 SMALL ONION, CHOPPED

2 TBSP SOY SAUCE

2 TBSP RICE WINE

½ TSP THAI SEVEN-SPICE POWDER

2 TBSP CLEAR HONEY

1 TBSP SESAME OIL

TO GARNISH

LEMON TWISTS

TO SERVE

ORANGE WEDGES

SERVES 4

Place the ribs in a wide roasting tin, cover loosely with foil and cook in a preheated oven, 180°C/350°F/Gas Mark 4, for 30 minutes.

Meanwhile, remove any pips from the lemon and orange, and place the fruits in a food processor, together with the ginger, garlic, onion, soy sauce, rice wine, seven-spice powder, honey and sesame oil. Process until smooth.

Pour off any fat from the spare ribs, then spoon the puréed mixture over the spare ribs.

Toss the ribs to coat evenly. Return the ribs to the oven, increase the temperature to 200°C/400°F/Gas Mark 6 and roast, turning and basting them occasionally, for about 40 minutes or until golden brown. Garnish with lemon twists and serve hot with orange wedges.

LAMB WITH BALSAMIC AND ROSEMARY MARINADE

6 RACKS OF LAMB,
EACH WITH 3 CUTLETS

SERVES 6

MARINADE

3 TBSP CHOPPED FRESH ROSEMARY

1 SMALL ONION, FINELY CHOPPED

3 TBSP OLIVE OIL

1 TBSP BALSAMIC VINEGAR

1 TBSP LEMON JUICE

SALT AND BLACK PEPPER

TO GARNISH

FRESH ROSEMARY SPRIGS

Put the lamb in a large, shallow dish and sprinkle with the chopped rosemary and onion. Whisk together the olive oil, balsamic vinegar and lemon juice and season with salt and pepper.

Pour the balsamic mixture over the lamb, turning well to coat. Cover with clingfilm and set aside in a cool place to marinate for 1–2 hours.

Drain the lamb, reserving the marinade. Grill the racks, on a medium hot barbecue, brushing frequently with the reserved marinade, for 8–10 minutes on each side. Serve garnished with rosemary sprigs.

Alternative Cooking Method

Place the lamb under a preheated grill, for 10-12 minutes, depending of the thickness of the meat, or until cooked through. Cooking times may be increased slightly as this method of cooking does not generate the high heat of a barbecue. You therefore will need to look for visual signs that the food is cooked to your liking.

PORK RIBS WITH
PLUM SAUCE

900 G/2 LB PORK SPARE RIBS

2 TBSP SUNFLOWER OIL

1 TSP SESAME OIL

2 CLOVES GARLIC, CRUSHED

2.5 CM/1 INCH PIECE ROOT GINGER,
GRATED

150 ML/¼ PINT PLUM SAUCE

2 TBSP DRY SHERRY

2 TBSP HOISIN SAUCE

2 TBSP SOY SAUCE

TO GARNISH

4–6 SPRING ONIONS

SERVES 4

To prepare the garnish, trim the spring onions to about
7.5 cm/3 inches long. Slice both ends into thin strips, leaving
the onion intact in the centre.

Put the spring onions into a bowl of iced water for at least
30 minutes until the ends start to curl up. Leave them in the
water and set aside until required.

If you buy the spare ribs in a single piece, cut them into individual
ribs. Bring a large pan of water to the boil and add the ribs. Cook
for 5 minutes, then drain thoroughly.

Heat the oils in a pan, add the garlic and ginger and cook gently
for 1–2 minutes. Stir in the plum sauce, sherry, hoisin and soy
sauce and heat through.

Brush the sauce over the pork ribs. Barbecue over hot coals for
5–10 minutes, then move to a cooler part of the barbecue for a
further 15–20 minutes, basting with the remaining sauce. Garnish
and serve hot.

DEEP-FRIED SPARE RIBS

8-10 FINGER SPARE RIBS

1 TSP FIVE-SPICE POWDER OR

1 TBSP MILD CURRY POWDER

1 TBSP RICE WINE OR DRY SHERRY

1 EGG

2 TBSP FLOUR

VEGETABLE OIL, FOR DEEP-FRYING

1 TSP FINELY SHREDDED
SPRING ONIONS

1 TSP FINELY SHREDDED FRESH
GREEN OR RED HOT CHILLIES,
SEEDED

SALT AND PEPPER

TO SERVE

SPICY SALT AND PEPPER

SERVES 4

Chop the ribs into 3-4 small pieces. Place the ribs in a bowl with salt, pepper, five-spice or curry powder and the wine. Turn to coat the ribs in the spices and leave to marinate for 1-2 hours.

Mix the egg and flour together to make a batter. Dip the ribs in the batter one by one to coat well.

Heat the oil in a preheated wok until smoking. Deep-fry the ribs for 4-5 minutes, then remove with chopsticks or a slotted spoon and drain on kitchen paper.

Reheat the oil over a high heat and deep-fry the ribs once more for another minute. Remove and drain again on kitchen paper.

Pour 1 tablespoon of the hot oil over the spring onions and chillies and leave for 30-40 seconds. Serve the ribs with Spicy Salt and Pepper, garnished with the shredded spring onions and chillies.

SPARE RIBS

900 G/2 LB PORK SPARE RIBS

2 TBSP DARK SOY SAUCE

3 TBSP HOISIN SAUCE

1 TBSP CHINESE RICE WINE OR
DRY SHERRY

PINCH OF CHINESE FIVE SPICE
POWDER

2 TSP DARK BROWN SUGAR

¼ TSP CHILLI SAUCE

2 GARLIC CLOVES, CRUSHED

TO GARNISH

CORIANDER SPRIGS

SERVES 4

Cut the spare ribs into separate pieces if they are joined together. If desired, you can chop them into 5 cm/2-inch lengths, using a cleaver.

Mix together the soy sauce, hoisin sauce, Chinese rice wine or sherry, Chinese five spice powder, dark brown sugar, chilli sauce and garlic in a large bowl.

Place the ribs in a shallow dish and pour the mixture over them, turning to coat them well. Cover and marinate in the refrigerator, turning the ribs from time to time, for at least 1 hour.

Remove the ribs from the marinade and arrange them in a single layer on a wire rack placed over a roasting tin half filled with warm water. Brush with the marinade, reserving the remainder.

Cook in a preheated oven, at 180°C/350°F/Gas Mark 4, for 30 minutes. Remove the roasting tin from the oven and turn the ribs over. Brush with the remaining marinade and return to the oven for a further 30 minutes, or until cooked through. Transfer to a warmed serving dish, garnish with the coriander sprigs and serve immediately.

BARBECUE RACK OF RIBS

2 RACKS OF PORK RIBS,
ABOUT 650 G/1 LB 7 OZ EACH
VEGETABLE OIL, FOR BRUSHING

SERVES 4-6

FOR THE TENNESSEE RUB
1 TBSP GROUND CUMIN
1 TSP GARLIC SALT
½ TSP GROUND CINNAMON
½ TSP DRY ENGLISH MUSTARD
POWDER
½ TSP GROUND CORIANDER
1 TSP DRIED MIXED HERBS
⅛ TSP CAYENNE PEPPER,
OR TO TASTE

**FOR THE BOURBON BARBECUE
SAUCE**
1 TBSP SUNFLOWER OR
GROUNDNUT OIL
½ ONION, FINELY CHOPPED
2 LARGE GARLIC CLOVES,
VERY FINELY CHOPPED
70 G/2 ½ OZ SOFT DARK BROWN
SUGAR
1 TBSP DRY ENGLISH MUSTARD
POWDER
1 TSP GROUND CUMIN
2 TBSP TOMATO PURÉE
6 TBSP BOURBON
2 TBSP WORCESTERSHIRE SAUCE
2 TBSP APPLE OR WHITE WINE
VINEGAR
FEW DROPS OF HOT PEPPER
SAUCE, TO TASTE

A day ahead, mix all the ingredients for the rub together in a small bowl. Rub the mixture onto both sides of the ribs, then cover and leave them to marinate in the refrigerator overnight.

To make the barbecue sauce, heat the oil in a saucepan over a medium-high heat. Add the onion and garlic and cook for 5 minutes, stirring frequently, or until the onion is soft. Stir in the remaining sauce ingredients. Slowly bring to the boil, stirring to dissolve the sugar, then reduce the heat and simmer, uncovered, for 30 minutes–1 hour, stirring occasionally, until dark brown and very thick. Leave to cool, then cover and chill until required.

When ready to barbecue, heat the coals until they are glowing. Brush the barbecue rack with a little oil. Put the ribs onto the rack and cook, turning frequently, for 40 minutes, or until the meat feels tender. If they appear to be drying out, brush with water.

Remove the ribs from the barbecue and cut them into 1- or 2-rib portions. Return the rib portions to the barbecue and brush with the sauce. Cook the ribs, turning frequently and basting generously with the sauce, for a further 10 minutes, or until they are dark brown and glossy. Serve with a bowl of the hot leftover sauce for dipping – and plenty of paper serviettes for sticky fingers!

BITE-SIZED BARBECUED SPARE RIBS

SAUCE

50 ML/2 FL OZ PLUM, HOISIN,
SWEET & SOUR OR DUCK SAUCE

1 TSP BROWN SUGAR

1 TBSP TOMATO KETCHUP

PINCH OF GARLIC POWDER

2 TBSP DARK SOY SAUCE

1 KG/2 LB 4OZ SPARE RIBS,
CHOPPED
INTO 5 CM/2 INCH PIECES

TO GARNISH

3 TBSP FRESH, TORN CORIANDER

SERVES 4

Preheat the oven to 190°C/375°F/Gas Mark 5.

To make the sauce, combine the plum or other sauce, brown sugar, ketchup, garlic powder and soy sauce in a large mixing bowl.

Add the spare ribs to the sauce and stir to coat them thoroughly. Transfer to a metal roasting pan and arrange in a single layer.

Place the roasting pan in the oven and cook the ribs for 20 minutes, or until they are cooked through and sticky. Arrange on a large platter and serve immediately, garnished with coriander.

SPARERIBS IN A SWEET-
AND-SOUR SAUCE

450 G/1 LB SPARERIBS, CUT INTO
BITE-SIZED PIECES

VEGETABLE OR GROUNDNUT OIL,
FOR DEEP-FRYING

FOR THE MARINADE

2 TSP LIGHT SOY SAUCE

½ TSP SALT

PINCH OF WHITE PEPPER

FOR THE SAUCE

3 TBSP WHITE RICE VINEGAR

2 TBSP SUGAR

1 TBSP LIGHT SOY SAUCE

1 TBSP TOMATO KETCHUP

1½ TBSP VEGETABLE OR
GROUNDNUT OIL

1 GREEN PEPPER,
ROUGHLY CHOPPED

1 SMALL ONION,
ROUGHLY CHOPPED

1 SMALL CARROT, FINELY SLICED

½ TSP FINELY CHOPPED GARLIC

½ TSP FINELY CHOPPED GINGER

100 G/3½ OZ PINEAPPLE CHUNKS

SERVES 4

Combine the marinade ingredients in a bowl with the pork and marinate for at least 20 minutes.

Heat enough oil for deep-frying in a wok, deep-fat fryer or large heavy-based saucepan until it reaches 180-190°C/350–375°F, or until a cube of bread browns in 30 seconds. Deep-fry the spareribs for 8 minutes. Drain and set aside.

To prepare the sauce, first mix together the vinegar, sugar, light soy sauce and ketchup. Set aside.

In a preheated wok or deep pan, heat 1 tablespoon of the oil and stir-fry the pepper, onion and carrot for 2 minutes. Remove and set aside.

In the clean preheated wok or deep pan, heat the remaining oil and stir-fry the garlic and ginger until fragrant. Add the vinegar mixture. Bring back to the boil and add the pineapple cubes. Finally add the spareribs and the pepper, onion and carrot. Stir until warmed through and serve immediately.

PORK RIBS BRAISED IN SOY SAUCE

600 G/1 LB 5 OZ PORK RIBS,
CUT INTO BITE-SIZED PIECES

1 TBSP DARK SOY SAUCE

1 WHOLE HEAD OF GARLIC

2 TBSP VEGETABLE OR
GROUNDNUT OIL OR LARD

1 CINNAMON STICK

2 STAR ANISE

3 TBSP LIGHT SOY SAUCE

55 G/2 OZ ROCK SUGAR

175 ML/6 FL OZ WATER

SERVES 4

Marinate the pork ribs in the dark soy sauce for at least 20 minutes.

Break the garlic head into cloves, leaving the individual skins intact.

In a preheated wok or deep pan, heat the oil and stir-fry the garlic cloves for 1 minute. Toss in the cinnamon and star anise and stir for a further minute. Stir in the pork. When the meat is beginning to brown, stir in the light soy sauce, sugar and water and stir until the sugar is dissolved. Simmer gently, uncovered, for 30 minutes, stirring frequently. Cover and simmer for 60–75 minutes until the meat is cooked through and the gravy thick and concentrated.

5 SIDES

It's hard to imagine roast beef without roast potatoes or steak without chips, but as well as these traditional accompaniments, this chapter is full of imaginative ideas for vegetables and salads to serve with steaks, chops, roasts and ribs. What could be tastier than Roasted Garlic Mashed Potatoes (see page 222) with roast lamb, Chargrilled Vegetables with Creamy Pesto (see page 220) with veal chops or Tropical Rice Salad (see page 226) with griddled pork? From Hush Puppies (see page 230) to Refried Beans (see page 228) and from Coleslaw (see page 242) to Chef's Salad (see page 240), you're sure to find the perfect partner for your meaty main dish.

PERFECT ROAST
POTATOES

1.3 KG/3 LB LARGE FLOURY
POTATOES, SUCH AS
KING EDWARDS, MARIS PIPER OR
DESIRÉE, PEELED AND
CUT INTO EVEN-SIZED CHUNKS

SALT

3 TBSP DRIPPING, GOOSE FAT,
DUCK FAT OR OLIVE OIL

SERVES 6

Preheat the oven to 220ºC/425ºF/Gas Mark 7.

Cook the potatoes in a large saucepan of boiling salted water over a medium heat, covered, for 5–7 minutes. They will still be firm. Remove from the heat.

Meanwhile, add the fat to a roasting tin and place in the hot oven.

Drain the potatoes well and return them to the saucepan. Cover with the lid and firmly shake the pan so that the surface of the potatoes is roughened to help give a much crisper texture.

Remove the roasting tin from the oven and carefully tip the potatoes into the hot oil. Baste them to ensure they are all coated with the oil.

Roast at the top of the oven for 45–50 minutes until they are browned all over and thoroughly crisp. Turn the potatoes and baste again only once during the process or the crunchy edges will be destroyed.

Carefully transfer the potatoes from the roasting tin into a hot serving dish. Sprinkle with a little salt and serve at once. Any leftovers (although this is most unlikely) are delicious cold.

CHARGRILLED VEGETABLES WITH
CREAMY PESTO

1 RED ONION

1 FENNEL BULB

4 BABY AUBERGINES

4 BABY COURGETTES

1 ORANGE PEPPER

1 RED PEPPER

2 BEEF TOMATOES

2 TBSP OLIVE OIL

SALT AND PEPPER

CREAMY PESTO

55 G/2 OZ FRESH BASIL LEAVES

15 G/½ OZ PINE KERNELS

1 GARLIC CLOVE

PINCH OF COARSE SEA SALT

25 G/1 OZ FRESHLY GRATED
PARMESAN CHEESE

50 ML/2 FL OZ EXTRA-VIRGIN
OLIVE OIL

150 ML/5 FL OZ NATURAL
GREEK YOGURT

TO GARNISH

1 FRESH BASIL SPRIG

SERVES 4

Preheat the barbecue. To make the creamy pesto, place the basil, pine kernels, garlic and sea salt in a mortar and pound to a paste with a pestle. Gradually work in the Parmesan cheese, then gradually stir in the oil. Place the yogurt in a small serving bowl and stir in 3–4 tablespoons of the pesto mixture. Cover with clingfilm and leave to chill in the refrigerator until required. Store any leftover pesto mixture in a screw-top jar in the refrigerator.

Prepare the vegetables. Cut the onion and fennel bulb into wedges, trim the aubergines and courgettes, deseed and halve the peppers and cut the tomatoes in half. Brush the vegetables with oil and season to taste with salt and pepper.

Cook the aubergines and peppers over hot coals for 3 minutes, then add the courgettes, onion and tomatoes and cook, turning occasionally and brushing with more oil if necessary, for a further 5 minutes. Transfer to a large serving plate and serve immediately with the pesto, garnished with a basil sprig.

Alternative Cooking Method
Preheat the griddle pan over a high heat. Cook the sliced vegetables in turn, griddling until the skins are slightly charred and the flesh is soft (about 2 minutes on each side), brushing with oil if necessary.

ROASTED GARLIC MASHED POTATOES

2 WHOLE BULBS OF GARLIC

1 TBSP OLIVE OIL

900 G/2 LB FLOURY POTATOES, PEELED

125 ML/4 FL OZ MILK

55 G/2 OZ BUTTER

SALT AND PEPPER

SERVES 4

Preheat the oven to 180°C/350°F/Gas Mark 4.

Separate the garlic cloves, place on a large piece of foil and drizzle with the oil. Wrap the garlic in the foil and roast in the oven for about 1 hour, or until very tender. Leave to cool slightly.

Twenty minutes before the end of the cooking time, cut the potatoes into chunks, then cook in salted boiling water for about 15 minutes, or until tender.

Meanwhile, squeeze the cooled garlic cloves out of their skins and push through a sieve, into a saucepan. Add the milk, butter, salt and pepper and heat gently, until the butter has melted.

Drain the cooked potatoes, then mash in the pan until smooth. Pour in the garlic mixture and heat gently, stirring, until the ingredients are combined. Serve hot.

CORNSTICKS

SUNFLOWER OIL, FOR OILING

175 G/6 OZ YELLOW CORNMEAL

115 G/4 OZ PLAIN FLOUR, SIFTED

1½–2 TBSP CASTER SUGAR,
TO TASTE

2½ TSP BAKING POWDER

¾ TSP SALT

5 SPRING ONIONS,
FINELY CHOPPED

250 ML/9 FL OZ MILK

1 EGG

TO SERVE

40 G/1½ OZ BUTTER, MELTED

MAKES 14

Preheat the oven to 220°C/425°F/Gas Mark 7. Generously brush two 7-stick moulds with oil and place them in the oven while it heats.

Do not start mixing the cornmeal batter until the oven has reached the correct temperature. Stir the cornmeal, flour, sugar, baking powder and salt together in a bowl, then stir in the spring onions. Make a well in the centre.

Mix the milk, egg and butter together in a jug, then stir into the dry ingredients until just mixed. Do not over-mix.

Remove the hot moulds from the oven and divide the cornmeal batter between them, filling each mould about three-quarters full. Return the moulds to the oven and bake for 20–25 minutes, or until risen and each cornstick is coming away from the side of the mould. A wooden cocktail stick inserted into the centre should come out clean.

Leave the cornsticks to stand for 1 minute, then use a round-bladed knife to ease them out of the moulds. Serve at once with butter for spreading over the cornsticks.

TROPICAL
RICE SALAD

115 G/4 OZ LONG-GRAIN RICE

SALT AND PEPPER

4 SPRING ONIONS

225 G/8 OZ CANNED PINEAPPLE
PIECES IN NATURAL JUICE

200 G/7 OZ CANNED SWEETCORN,
DRAINED

2 RED PEPPERS,
DESEEDED AND DICED

3 TBSP SULTANAS

DRESSING

1 TBSP GROUNDNUT OIL

1 TBSP HAZELNUT OIL

1 TBSP LIGHT SOY SAUCE

1 GARLIC CLOVE, FINELY CHOPPED

1 TSP CHOPPED FRESH ROOT GINGER

SERVES 4

Cook the rice in a large saucepan of lightly salted boiling water for 15 minutes, or until tender. Drain thoroughly and rinse under cold running water. Place the rice in a large serving bowl.

Using a sharp knife, finely chop the spring onions. Drain the pineapple pieces, reserving the juice in a jug. Add the pineapple pieces, sweetcorn, red peppers, chopped spring onions and sultanas to the rice and mix lightly.

Add all the dressing ingredients to the reserved pineapple juice, whisking well, and season to taste with salt and pepper. Pour the dressing over the salad and toss until the salad is thoroughly coated. Serve immediately.

REFRIED BEANS

6–8 TBSP SUNFLOWER OR CORN OIL
OR 85–115 G/3–4 OZ LARD
1 ONION, FINELY CHOPPED
1 QUANTITY OF FRIJOLES

TO SERVE
FRIED TORTILLAS

SERVES 6

Heat 2 tablespoons of the sunflower oil in a large, heavy-based frying pan. Add the chopped onion and cook, stirring occasionally, for 5 minutes, or until softened. Add one-quarter of the Frijoles.

Mash the Frijoles with a potato masher until well broken up. Add more Frijoles and more oil and mash again. Continue adding Frijoles and oil until all the beans have been incorporated and have formed a solid paste.

Cut the tortillas into quarters. Transfer the refried beans on to a warmed serving dish, shaping the paste into one large roll, and serve immediately, surrounded with the tortilla quarters.

HUSH PUPPIES

250 G/9 OZ YELLOW CORNMEAL

70 G/2½ OZ PLAIN FLOUR, SIFTED

1 SMALL ONION, FINELY CHOPPED

1 TBSP SUGAR

2 TSP BAKING POWDER

½ TSP SALT

175 ML/6 FL OZ MILK

1 EGG, BEATEN

SUNFLOWER OIL, FOR DEEP-FRYING

MAKES ABOUT 36

Stir the cornmeal, flour, onion, sugar, baking powder and salt together in a bowl and make a well in the centre.

Beat the milk and egg together in a jug, then pour into the dry ingredients and stir until a thick batter forms.

Heat at least 5 cm/2 inches of oil in a deep frying pan or saucepan over a high heat until the temperature reaches 180–190°C/350–375°F, or until a cube of bread browns in 30 seconds.

Drop as many teaspoonfuls of the batter as will fit without overcrowding the pan and cook, stirring constantly, until the hush puppies puff up and turn golden.

Remove the hush puppies from the oil with a slotted spoon and drain on kitchen paper. Reheat the oil, if necessary, and cook the remaining batter. Serve hot.

CANDIED SWEET POTATOES

675 G/1 LB 8 OZ SWEET POTATOES, SLICED

40 G/1½ OZ BUTTER

1 TBSP LIME JUICE

75 G/2¾ OZ SOFT DARK BROWN SUGAR

1 TBSP BRANDY

GRATED RIND OF 1 LIME

TO GARNISH

LIME WEDGES

SERVES 6

Cook the sweet potatoes in a large, heavy-based saucepan of boiling water for 5 minutes, or until softened. To test if the potatoes are soft, prick with a fork. Remove the sweet potatoes with a slotted spoon and drain thoroughly.

Melt the butter in a large frying pan. Add the lime juice and sugar and heat gently, stirring, to dissolve the sugar.

Stir the sweet potatoes and the brandy into the sugar and lime juice mixture. Cook over a low heat for 10 minutes, or until the potato slices are cooked through.

Sprinkle the lime rind over the top of the sweet potatoes and mix well.

Transfer the candied sweet potatoes to a large, warmed serving plate. Garnish with lime wedges and serve immediately.

BLACK BEAN NACHOS

225 G/8 OZ DRIED BLACK BEANS,
OR CANNED BLACK BEANS,
DRAINED AND RINSED

175–225 G/6–8 OZ GRATED CHEESE,
SUCH AS CHEDDAR, FONTINA,
PECORINO, ASIAGO OR
A COMBINATION

ABOUT ¼ TSP CUMIN SEEDS OR
GROUND CUMIN

ABOUT 4 TBSP SOURED CREAM

THINLY SLICED PICKLED
JALAPEÑOS (OPTIONAL)

1 TBSP CHOPPED FRESH CORIANDER

HANDFUL OF SHREDDED LETTUCE

TO SERVE

TORTILLA CHIPS

SERVES 4

If using dried black beans, place them in a bowl and add water to cover. Set aside to soak overnight, then drain. Put in a pan, cover with water and bring to the boil. Boil for 10 minutes, then reduce the heat and simmer for about 1½ hours until tender. Drain well.

Spread the cooked or canned beans in the base of a shallow ovenproof dish, then sprinkle the cheese over the top. Sprinkle with cumin to taste.

Bake in a preheated oven, 190°C/375°F/Gas Mark 5, for 10–15 minutes or until the beans are cooked through and the cheese is bubbling and melted.

Remove the beans and cheese from the oven and spoon the soured cream on top. Add the jalapeños, if using, and sprinkle with fresh coriander and lettuce.

Arrange the tortilla chips around the beans, sticking them into the mixture. Serve the nachos at once.

GARLIC POTATO WEDGES

3 LARGE BAKING POTATOES,
SCRUBBED

4 TBSP OLIVE OIL

2 TBSP BUTTER

2 GARLIC CLOVES, CHOPPED

1 TBSP CHOPPED, FRESH ROSEMARY

1 TBSP CHOPPED FRESH PARSLEY

1 TBSP CHOPPED FRESH THYME

SALT AND PEPPER

SERVES 4

Bring a large pan of water to the boil, add the potatoes and parboil them for 10 minutes. Drain the potatoes, refresh under cold water and then drain them again thoroughly.

Transfer the potatoes to a chopping board. When the potatoes are cold enough to handle, cut them into thick wedges, but do not peel.

Heat the oil and butter in a small pan together with the garlic. Cook gently until the garlic begins to brown, then remove the pan from the heat.

Stir the herbs and seasoning into the mixture in the pan.

Brush the herb and butter mixture all over the potato wedges.

Barbecue the potatoes over hot coals for 10-15 minutes, brushing liberally with any of the remaining herb and butter mixture, or until the potato wedges are just tender.

Transfer the garlic potato wedges to a warm serving plate and serve as a starter or as a side dish.

Alternative Cooking Method

Preheat the oven to 220°C/ 425°F/Gas Mark 7. Place wedges into a roasting tin and cook for 35-45 minutes until golden and crispy.

CORN-ON-THE-COB

4 CORN COBS, WITH HUSKS

100 G/3½ OZ BUTTER

1 TBSP CHOPPED FRESH PARSLEY

1 TSP CHOPPED FRESH CHIVES

1 TSP CHOPPED FRESH THYME

GRATED RIND OF 1 LEMON

SALT AND PEPPER

SERVES 4

Preheat the barbecue. To prepare the corn cobs, peel back the husks and remove the silken hairs. Fold back the husks and secure them in place with string if necessary.

Blanch the corn cobs in a large saucepan of boiling water for 5 minutes. Remove the corn cobs with a slotted spoon and drain thoroughly. Cook the corn cobs over medium hot coals for 20–30 minutes, turning frequently.

Meanwhile, soften the butter and beat in the parsley, chives, thyme, lemon rind and salt and pepper to taste. Transfer the corn cobs to serving plates, remove the string and pull back the husks. Serve each with a generous portion of herb butter.

Alternative Cooking Method
Cook the cobs in boiling water or steam for 10-12 minutes. When cooked the kernels should feel tender when pierced.

CHEF'S SALAD

1 ICEBERG LETTUCE, SHREDDED

175 G/6 OZ COOKED HAM,
CUT INTO THIN STRIPS

175 G/6 OZ COOKED TONGUE,
CUT INTO THIN STRIPS

350 G/12 OZ COOKED CHICKEN,
CUT INTO THIN STRIPS

175 G/6 OZ GRUYÈRE CHEESE

4 TOMATOES, QUARTERED

3 HARD-BOILED EGGS, SHELLED
AND QUARTERED

400 ML/14 FL OZ THOUSAND
ISLAND DRESSING

SERVES 6

Arrange the lettuce on a large serving platter. Arrange the cold meat decoratively on top.

Cut the Gruyère cheese into batons.

Arrange the cheese batons over the salad, and the tomato and egg quarters around the edge of the platter. Serve the salad immediately, and serve the dressing separately.

COLESLAW

SERVES 4-6

225 G/8 OZ WHITE CABBAGE,
CORED AND GRATED

225 G/8 OZ CARROTS, PEELED AND
GRATED

25 G/1 OZ SUGAR

3 TBSP CIDER VINEGAR

5 TBSP DOUBLE CREAM,
LIGHTLY WHIPPED

2 PICKLED GREEN OR
RED PEPPERS, DRAINED AND
THINLY SLICED (OPTIONAL)

4 TBSP FINELY CHOPPED FRESH
PARSLEY

SALT AND PEPPER

Combine the cabbage, carrots, sugar, vinegar, a large pinch of salt and pepper to taste in a large bowl, tossing the ingredients together. Cover and leave to chill for 1 hour.

Stir all the ingredients together well. Lightly stir in the whipped cream and the pickled peppers, if using. Taste and add extra sugar, vinegar or salt, if desired. Sprinkle over the parsley and serve at once. Alternatively, cover and chill until required.

POTATO SKINS WITH GUACAMOLE

4 LARGE BAKING POTATOES

2 TSP OLIVE OIL

COARSE SEA SALT AND PEPPER

GUACAMOLE DIP

175 G/6 OZ RIPE AVOCADO

1 TBSP LEMON JUICE

2 RIPE, FIRM TOMATOES,
CHOPPED FINELY

1 TSP GRATED LEMON RIND

100 G/3½ OZ LOW-FAT SOFT
CHEESE WITH HERBS AND GARLIC

4 SPRING ONIONS,
CHOPPED FINELY

A FEW DROPS OF TABASCO SAUCE

SALT AND PEPPER

TO GARNISH

CHOPPED FRESH CHIVES

SERVES 4

Bake the potatoes in a preheated oven at 200°C/400°F/Gas Mark 6 for 1¼ hours. Remove from the oven and allow to cool for 30 minutes. Reset the oven to 220°C/425°F/Gas Mark 7.

Halve the potatoes lengthwise and scoop out 2 tablespoons of the flesh. Slice in half again. Place on a baking tray and brush the flesh side lightly with oil. Sprinkle with salt and pepper. Bake for a further 25 minutes until golden and crisp.

To make the guacamole dip, mash the avocado with the lemon juice. Add the remaining ingredients and mix.

Drain the potato skins on paper towels and transfer to a warmed serving platter. Garnish with chives. Pile the avocado mixture into a serving bowl.

SPICY RICE

3 TBSP OLIVE OIL

6 SPRING ONIONS, CHOPPED

1 CELERY STICK, FINELY CHOPPED

3 GARLIC CLOVES,
FINELY CHOPPED

2 GREEN PEPPERS,
DESEEDED AND CHOPPED

SWEETCORN KERNELS,
CUT FROM 1 CORN ON THE COB

2 FRESH MILD GREEN CHILLIES,
DESEEDED AND FINELY CHOPPED

250 G/9 OZ LONG-GRAIN RICE

2 TSP GROUND CUMIN

600 ML/1 PINT CHICKEN OR
VEGETABLE STOCK

2 TBSP CHOPPED FRESH CORIANDER

SALT AND PEPPER

TO GARNISH

FRESH CORIANDER SPRIGS

SERVES 4

Heat the oil in a large, heavy-based saucepan over a medium heat. Add the spring onions, celery and garlic and cook for 5 minutes, or until softened. Add the peppers, sweetcorn and chillies and cook for 5 minutes.

Add the rice and cumin and cook, stirring to coat the grains in the oil, for 2 minutes.

Stir in the stock and half the chopped coriander and bring to the boil. Reduce the heat, cover and simmer for 15 minutes, or until nearly all the liquid has been absorbed and the rice is just tender.

Remove from the heat and fluff up with a fork. Stir in the remaining chopped coriander and season to taste with salt and pepper. Leave to stand, covered, for 5 minutes before serving. Serve garnished with coriander sprigs.

HOME-MADE OVEN CHIPS

450 G/1 LB POTATOES, PEELED

2 TBSP SUNFLOWER OIL

SALT AND PEPPER

SERVES 4

Preheat the oven to 200°C/400°F/Gas Mark 6.

Cut the potatoes into thick, even-sized chips. Rinse them under cold running water and then dry well on a clean tea towel. Put in a bowl, add the oil and toss together until coated.

Spread the chips on a baking sheet and cook in the oven for 40–45 minutes, turning once, until golden. Add salt and pepper to taste and serve hot.

POTATO, ROCKET AND MOZZARELLA SALAD

650 G/1 LB 7 OZ SMALL
NEW POTATOES
125 G/4½ OZ ROCKET LEAVES
150 G/5½ OZ FIRM MOZZARELLA
1 LARGE PEAR
1 TBSP LEMON JUICE
SALT AND PEPPER

DRESSING
3 TBSP EXTRA-VIRGIN OLIVE OIL
1½ TBSP WHITE WINE VINEGAR
1 TSP SUGAR
PINCH OF MUSTARD POWDER

SERVES 4

Bring a saucepan of salted water to the boil. Add the potatoes, reduce the heat and cook for about 15 minutes, or until tender. Remove from the heat, drain and set aside to cool.

When the potatoes are cool, halve them and place them in a large salad bowl. Wash and drain the rocket leaves, cut the mozzarella into cubes, and wash, trim and slice the pear. Add them to the bowl along with the lemon juice. Season with salt and pepper.

To make the dressing, mix together the oil, vinegar, sugar and mustard powder. Pour the dressing over the salad and toss all the ingredients together until they are well coated. Serve at once.

RÖSTI

450 G/1 LB FLOURY POTATOES

1 MEDIUM ONION, GRATED

SALT AND PEPPER

FAT FOR SHALLOW FRYING

SERVES 4

Wash the potatoes, but do not peel them. Place in a large pan, cover with water and bring to the boil, covered, over a high heat. Reduce the heat and simmer for about 10 minutes, until the potatoes are just beginning to soften. Be careful not to overcook.

Drain the potatoes. Leave to cool, then peel and grate coarsely. Mix the grated onion with the potatoes. Season the mixture with salt and pepper.

Heat the oil or fat in a heavy-based frying pan and spoon in the potato mixture. The rösti can be as thick or as thin as you like, and can be made into one large cake or several individual ones.

Cook over a high heat for about 5 minutes, until the bottom is golden, then turn and cook until the second side is brown and crispy. Remove from the heat, drain and serve.

INDEX